BOOKS BY DONALD FINKEL

Selected Shorter Poems   1987

The Wake of the Electron   1987

The Detachable Man   1984

What Manner of Beast   1981

Endurance and *Going Under*   1978

A Mote in Heaven's Eye   1975

Adequate Earth   1972

The Garbage Wars   1970

Answer Back   1968

A Joyful Noise   1966

Simeon   1964

The Clothing's New Emperor   1959
(IN POETS OF TODAY VI)

Selected Shorter Poems

Donald Finkel

ATHENEUM

PUBLISHERS

115 Fifth Avenue　　　　　　　　*New York, N.Y. 10003*

Title: SELECTED SHORTER POEMS
Author: Donald Finkel
Publication Date: May 27 1987
Price: Hardcover: $21.00
　　　 Paperback: $12.95
ISBN: Hardcover: 0-689-11854-4
　　　 Paperback: 0-689-11856-2

THIS BOOK *is sent to you with our com-*

pliments. Should you publish any men-

tion of it, we would be grateful for two

clippings of your article. Please do

not review the book before its

publication date.

Selected Shorter Poems

ATHENEUM   NEW YORK   1987

FOR HARRY

Contents

Contents

FROM A JOYFUL NOISE

Contents

FROM *THE GARBAGE WARS*

FROM *A MOTE IN HEAVEN'S EYE*

Contents

FROM *WHAT MANNER OF BEAST*

FROM *THE DETACHABLE MAN*

Contents

The Clothing's New Emperor

AN ESTHETIC OF IMITATION

Preferring 'resemblance to beauty,'
There were some who found more
Truth in Philoktetes' rotten legs
Than in the smooth buttocks
Of a hundred Venuses. There
Is something in certain events that
Drives one to repetition. The act
Is all; one says, this thing,
'Craftsmen, beggars, topers with rags,'
This thing.

        With cheeks of silver,
Silanion inlaid the pallor of Iokaste.
Not life, rather this thing, which bangs
Silver into the real. Not there, rather
Before, or beside: 'the morning
After the taking of Troy, Odysseus
After slaying the suitors.'

           Brother,
Nothing is real that has happened
Only once; and nothing can happen
Again, and still be true. One sings,
Not what was, but *that* it was;
What was true in flesh, is
Merely beautiful in silver.

HUNTING SONG

The fox he came lolloping, lolloping,
Lolloping. His eyes were bright,
His ears were high.
He was like death at the end of a string
When he came to the hollow
Log. He ran in one side
And out of the other. O
He was sly.

The hounds they came tumbling, tumbling,
Tumbling. Their heads were low,
Their eyes were red.
The sound of their breath was louder than death
When they came to the hollow
Log. They boiled at one end
But a bitch found the scent. O
They were mad.

The hunter came galloping, galloping,
Galloping. All damp was his mare
From her hooves to her mane.
His coat and his mouth were redder than death
When he came to the hollow
Log. He took in the rein
And over he went. O
He was fine.

The log he just lay there, alone in
The clearing. No fox nor hound
Nor mounted man
Saw his black round eyes in their perfect disguise
(As the ends of a hollow
Log). He watched death go through him,
Around him and over him. O
He was wise.

THE GREAT WAVE: HOKUSAI

But we will take the problem in its most obscure manifestation, and suppose that our spectator is an average Englishman. A trained observer, carefully hidden behind a screen, might notice a dilation in his eyes, even an intake of his breath, perhaps a grunt. HERBERT READ: *The Meaning of Art*

It is because the sea is blue,
Because Fuji is blue, because the bent blue
Men have white faces, like the snow
On Fuji, like the crest of the wave in the sky the color of their
Boats. It is because the air
Is full of writing, because the wave is still: that nothing
Will harm these frail strangers,
That high over Fuji in an earthcolored sky the fingers
Will not fall; and the blue men
Lean on the sea like snow, and the wave like a mountain leans
Against the sky.

          In the painter's sea
All fishermen are safe. All anger bends under his unity.
But the innocent bystander, he merely
'Walks round a corner, thinking of nothing': hidden
Behind a screen we hear his cry.
He stands half in and half out of the world; he is the men,
But he cannot see below Fuji
The shore the color of sky; he is the wave, he stretches
His claws against strangers. He is
Not safe, not even from himself. His world is flat.
He fishes a sea full of serpents, he rides his boat
Blindly from wave to wave toward Ararat.

BRAILLE

The hand of an emperor heavy
With rings, beading of rain
Under a black branch, a flat rose
Carved into a frame,
Illuminated monkish prose:
Raised on the bleak flesh, we see
The adorning welts of poetry.

The columns of the temple are
Fluted and ineffectual,
And angels on the altar bang
Unnecessary wings.
                    Yet braille
Embossings on the year may stir
The senses, and improve the view:
As through her flimsy dress the Spring
Lets her disturbing garters show.

ARCHAIC FIGURINE FROM NAYARIT

She has been pregnant for two thousand years
With something which, by now, she has
No intention of revealing. Out of eyes
Like coffee beans she contemplates
What certainly must be to her a hell
Of a change from the months when she was clean
And meaningful.

Her mouth is rounded with the taste of our
Apartments. From Cuzco to Culiacan
They have unearthed the likes of her, proving
She was no ordinary matron:
Her head is flat, her burden is ideal;
Two millenniums of pain
Have left her skull

Placid and unreal. She will not bear
Gods against our chaos. She has
Not chosen this. I don't know what she sees
In me: she has known stronger lovers.
However, I take shape slowly. Under her cool
Regard I shall, I think, in time,
Be beautiful.

THE CLOTHING'S NEW EMPEROR

Such as it is. Such as two men
Talking because there is nothing
Easier than to talk. All things
Momentary as that, as the flame

Between two mouths meeting
In simple speech, flame
Clothed in the commonest phrases,
Bent merely, as light bending

In water, and shaking. Such
As it is. Lips mouthing vowels
In a vacuum, as in a silent film,
Not empty, rather unheard speech,

Caught at the distance between
Two minds, talking because it is
Easy to talk. Nothing is
Given but the forms. They have seen

The clothes without the emperor.
Deceived by fleas, they see flesh
Under the shirt, blood rushing
Inside the sleeves and out of the collar.

TARGET PRACTICE

On the first day good enough father and son
Went out with the new gun
And rode for miles in Iowa.

No. That spring, city-bred and new to sun,
We went out in the car in Iowa
And parked at last between
Two farms and walked, through mud, to the place.

Neither is right, the fiction
Or the fact. It is as if
What happened were good enough, as if the place,
If I described it, might produce
Shoots between the wagon-ruts,
As the spring works, yearly, miracles in Iowa.
No poem grows anything.
The hands of words are tender,
False to work, as you and I were false, in Iowa,
To mud and gun, were neither
Farmer's son nor father,
Whose ancient secrets back away from words
Like huge and hungry birds
That have no use for song.

A poem is the least kind of honesty. Words
Have their sense and semblance.
When I saw, over the place,
The huge bird angling, I said, It's a hawk,
It's a hawk, and you could
Shoot then, at something,
Even if it was a crow we saw, and not a hawk
At all.

But a poem is the least
Kind of honesty. It's to subsist
In woods for weeks on weeds to tell your friends

How you and nature are like
That. One must, to speak
Directly, have, at first, something to say to friends,
To sons. That spring in Iowa
We shot skyward at the hawk,
The crow, in a copse between two farms. We hit
Nothing, I think, though three
Times the big bird suddenly,
For a silent moment, fell, as if we'd really hit
Him, then changed direction
And wheeled off, screaming.

We did not hit him, I think, and I don't know
If it was a hawk or a crow
We didn't hit that day,
Between two populated farms, and I don't know
Where the bullets finally
Went, or if they killed
Some farmer, maybe, or his son, someone who knew
Hunting, mud, knew guns, who
Spoke little, having little
To say, could tell a hawk from a crow, and knew
His father, maybe, the way you
Don't know me, or I know you.

LE JONGLEUR DE NOTRE-DAME

It runs something like this:
This is certainly not the age
For tragic figures, since

Who ever heard of a tragic
Figure getting a majority
In the popular elections?

Secondly, everybody is hip
These days: who is dumb
Enough to get himself killed

For a cause? Or the little
Fellow, kicking six copper
Balls and twelve knives with

His heels, before the Mother
Of God: the sweat gathers
On his brow. However,

He does not wish to appear
Ridiculous; his hands are free
At all times with a handker-

chief, should the Lady prefer
To remain on the altar.

GIVE WAY

Give way to the man coming at you:
He is probably organized, or he
Is a Mason, so much the worse
For you. The child ahead of you
Walks carefully, does not step
On a crack. She knows. Keep
Close to the buildings, stick
To the well-lit avenues, give way.

'Man that is born of woman is of
Few days, and full of trouble.
He cometh forth like a flower,
And is cut down: he fleeth also
As a shadow, and continueth not.'
Your path will be covered with cracks;
Beware of a tall man who will bring
Ill fortune; beware of a short man:
He will be armed.

          Or, better yet,
Organize, call meetings, make speeches,
Pay dues. With the dues, acquire
A public address system, and make
Louder speeches. Cast ballots, win.

If you will notice, now, the tall
Man, he tests the microphones,
The short man insures with his gun
The collection of dues; everyone
Is stepping between the cracks.
However, nobody is fully satisfied:
Keep close to the buildings, give way;
The man coming at you may be armed.

IN GRATITUDE

Small but adequate deaths
Try me at every turn;
What I do not kill myself
Dies while I look on:

The swallow I picked up under
His nest this morning, I tried
To feed all day with a dropper,
But tonight he died.

And how many times has a fly,
Kicking the death from his belly,
Pained me an instant, till I
Hit him more squarely?

And I am loath to remember
A lizard I kept in a can,
That cooked, while I dawdled at dinner,
In the afternoon sun.

Who mocked at me with the nestling,
And kept him alive all day
Nodding his head at something
I could not see?

Shall I let him know of my grief
Regarding the houseflies, seeing
What hurt me was not their death,
But merely their dying?

No matter. All things considered,
I thank whoever was kind
At least for the death of the lizard
While my back was turned.

OF ALL THE WAYS TO DIE

Ridiculous Midas broke his teeth on gold,
And the old fool repented.
The little princess resented
The pea: *then* they knew her. Folks in the old
Days made a regular profession of displeasure:
Castles were draughty
Arrangements, musty
Old tombs at best. Banging lances under the azure
Brought blue bruises, and later the fair lady
Gave out her favors
To the aching victor
From an icy bed. Ridiculous Midas beat his body
Against his gold sheets. The little princess tossed
All night on the pea.
Of all the ways to die,
To croak in a draughty castle is the best.

KING MIDAS HAS ASSES' EARS

Under his careful crown he keeps
His psyche safe, and every day
In a kingdom of eyes he makes his way.
Only at midnight when his subjects sleep
In easy ignorance he stands before
His mirror, running his soft ears
Through his hands. Below the stairs
Servants like recriminations stir
In their beds, and the night birds
Scream Ears, ears! in mounting minor thirds.

Nobody hears, but yet he royally must
Be shaved in the mornings, nightly undressed;
Sunlight through his window-blind commands
The drawing near of strange impolitic hands.
His valet knocks: now like a whore he suffers
The hands, the eyes, of an untimely lover.

The barber stands behind his chair
And works the secrets from his hair;
As in a dim confessional,
The secular professional
Passive uncomprehending ear
Hears more than it was meant to hear.

I am a king who tells you this. Just so,
I keep them under my hat, all day
My kingdom course, between the hands and eyes;
At night before my mirror watch them grow
Softer and taller. Yet cannot keep
My peace: it is not servants merely
Who run and tell. I tell them daily
When they cut my hair, drag up my steep
Stair ice, my laundry. I confide
To urchins in the street who clean my shoes,

Stretch on a couch each morning and accuse
Myself of murder, mayhem, fratricide.
I am a king who tells you this: they know
Us better than we know ourselves, and rightly so.

DRINKING SONG

For all those that travel in droves
Down Rhône or Rhine, between harsh
Alp and secret Pyrenees,
For all those that thumb the soft
French shore of the world, where
It is hard to know whether the beach
Slides into the sea, or sea laps
Shore, eliding blue over the smooth
Stones, smoothed by eliding tongue,
The soft français of sleep—for all
Those mothered by the sun, kissed
Or calmed by boys on bicycles, arms,
Arms entwining, in the beer-hall of baritone
Love:
       the final war marks
Time in the mountains, confused because
You are unconfused, afraid because
You have no fear, sobbing
In the wash of your laughter, which smoothes
The harsh Alp of the mind, and nudges
Apart the teeth of the Pyrenees.

OLD LADY WITH ROSARY ON THE BUS TO PUEBLA

Let me find my way to the beginning of this:
You count these beads so as to pray enough.
We ride toward these mountains as toward death,
Which in this clear air is further than you suppose.
(Coming down from Pompeii, the man told us,
The driver kept calling over his shoulder, If
We make this next one we will be all right.)

Or maybe it starts here: you count so as not
To pray too long. The mountains come to you
Over the driver's shoulder. Who wrought
This miracle in which we sit; who lifts you
So as to let, looming, the mountains slip
Under your prayers, under your barren lap?

Or is the beginning when you reach
The silver agony that by your thumb
Swings toward a fixity which hardly comes
But it is gone again, and you begin
To jog him gently through another death,
While you plead amnesty under your breath?

Nothing is first, since you begin again;
When is enough if once, for you, and twice
Are one and the same? (At the corrida his wife,
He whined to us, sat through the first three bulls,
Then dragged him out; so he missed the goring.)
O Chano, darling of the Plaza, how does it feel
When your number comes up, when you are turning
On the horn, as from the summit of an inverse hill
You look up a slope of sighs and death is a ring
Of eyes like beads flicking an endless string?

JACOB

I did not want his blessing. It was
The old hag drove me to it, her
Witching and wheedling. Let me
Tell you, I was scared, sweating
And stinking under the skins. The
Old man said, Jake, is it you? and
Out of my mouth, fawning, my
Mother's voice, natural to me as
Hate. But I tell you, it is easier
To love. That hairy ape; even in
The womb, he wrestled me tenderly.

I, who've learned woman's love,
Now I reap her harvest; who have
Crept between the dream and the
Acceptance, have now neither dream
Nor the acceptance. Now, in the
Desert, night is no colder than
His hate; my mother's love warms
Me less than the jackals, nosing
Me in the darkness. Now the old
Hag sits in the door, howling
Herself warm. The ape sweats
Anger under his red hair. Let
Me ask you, can I wrap the damn
Blessing around me for a blanket?

BLUEBEARD

With the first one it was simple;
It has never been so simple since.
Often as a child I found myself
By some whim sprawled out on
The floor. Once there, once dead,
The problem was merely to stay.

The same: the room, once entered,
Held no mystery. The problem was
To discover why one had entered
In the first place. Finding no
Answer, one could hardly leave
Without being seriously transformed.

As to the first, I have never been
Sure why I killed her. I remember
Passing the door, seeing it ajar;
I remember the odors of her fear,
The white questioning hands upon
My arm. I remember, through the door
Closing, her white face frozen in surprise.

Once done, it was clear enough, the only
Explanation was to do it again. I have
Always prided myself on my moral consistency.
It has never been so simple, since.

JUAN BELMONTE, TORERO

The first thing, I think, is a keen sense
Of the ridiculous. Before each corrida
To finger anew one's duties, one's motivations,
A housewife among suspicious vegetables.

Outside the mob shifts on its terrible
Haunches. It is strange: without them,
The whole thing is meaningless. The bull
Has more sense of his part. Many times I sit
Out there: I think to myself, how the hell
Can he do it? I see the bull tear out
Of the toril, and I am convinced that I should
Never be able to fight him.

                        How much easier
In the old days. In Tablada, naked and dripping
Under the moon, losing the bull in the darkness;
Then suddenly the white horns, like the arms
Of a bathing girl.

                        Each time they expected
More, and each time I had less to give.
Now I no longer remember what it was
I *meant* to give. The mob shakes its terrible
Hair. The old faenas are smoothed into
The sand. Glittering young men tread on it,
In their soft slippers and their bravery.

ODYSSEUS

It was better in the tents: Achilles
Scowling in the half-light, nudging
The armor with his naked toes. Or

Getting chased into the water, the
Tents collapsing, all howling Troy
About my ears, jabbing, pulling me

Down. To be sought after by a son,
It is to be dragged into youth
Again, seeking a girl on whom to

Sire a son; it is the whole damn thing
All over again. But to have done with
The wars, to have gotten home before

The suitors arrived, to have taken the
Short-cut across the years: what in hell
Could I have done with all that time?

DIONYSUS

Man, they just took me apart, the women
And all. The wine was their idea. High
Or low, they trundled me, never content:
A round of need and blood, then
Need again, binding me, slave to their loins.

Always something new, one town
After another: the tent cities, camel
Stink, outside in the night the jackals
Yipping. After, the land between the two
Rivers, the ones that flow backwards,
Whooping it up in Ur and Babylon.
And far as the Bactrian mountains,
Spreading the good word, pine wand
And vine leaf, lugging me like an idol.
What could a god do? Came finally winter,
Tore me limb from limb: a few months'
Breather, there under the decorous,
Moral snow.

                    But to be born again every spring:
Back through the Medes, past Gordium,
Wailing. A lousy taste every morning,
The she-goats frantic at my arms, dragging me
Into the reel. Past Sardis to the sea,
Glitter and gull-cry, Scios at horizon. Then
Northwards to Thrace, and the peninsula.

O the joy of the blood and the raw
Red flesh! In Thebes, the king my cousin,
Loving order, and lovesick Orpheus in Thrace,
Who rocked Hades with his harp: dead.
Dead, both of them, music and meaning.
All crumbs, scattered to sea-wind. The bread
Is gone, my body: now every spring
Five days they come and tell sad tales
To me of kings, and swill my blood.

THE HUNT OF THE UNICORN

A TAPESTRY IN FIVE ACTS

> *In the Unicorn series at the Cloisters in
> New York there are six tapestries and
> fragments of another. Five of these were in
> all probability made for Anne of Brittany
> in celebration of her marriage to Louis XII.
> The first and seventh tapestries, somewhat
> later in date than the others, may have
> been added to the original set when Francis I
> married Anne's daughter and heiress.*

PROLOGUE: *THE START OF THE HUNT*

All starts are false: even Francis,
Who bid the weavers add beginning
And end to a fabulous enough encounter,
Knew from his distance how all
Eminence falls into a plane, no
Rise, decline, only a continuous
Between, tasting of both.

                Certain
As a child, art from a thousand starts
Weaves one real as roses. Deep
In a millefoil Eden the young king
Poises between friends, anxious as his hounds,
As if the chase were not always to begin,
As if the Hamlet in his heart stayed
Not the spears, rough-hafted, from their course.

Caught between ages, human and divine,
The king and his companions, now as then,
Poise as to the sounding of a horn,
While stationed in the trees one servant calls,
Who probably has seen the unicorn.

ACT I: *THE UNICORN AT THE FOUNTAIN*

Beard matted in mammoth-dung,
Cain caught in a hell of sun
And sunstriped tigers with teeth
Of sun, and the mammoth
Stomping in the underbrush,
Knew in his animal guts that birth
Is the final destruction of Paradise.

And at the fountain of the heart
The virgin and the hunter wait,
The one with stealth and spear
And snare, the one by odor of desire,
To tempt the savior from his lair,
The lover springe in spite of fear.
Long since the serpent fouled and fled,
And who will keep the panther sweet,
Or save the blood-lipped lion
From his own thirst?
                    The lover-
Savior dips his horn,
The maiden and the panther drink,
The spearman toasts unto the king,
But who will heal the unicorn?

ACT II: *THE UNICORN TRIES TO ESCAPE*

Yet who has seen him? Who,
For that matter, the lion,
The panther, or the elephant, who hath
No knees, but like a child,
Fallen is helpless, and is safely killed.
And side by side, the dragon
And the basilisk, the amphisboena,
The salamander that lives in fire.

Part horse, part antelope; tail
Of a lion, some say, that from
That meek behind might lash
The felon with a hidden nail.
An horne of foure fote long,
As if two caught in an instant
Profile, fortunate metaphor
For Father and His Son
Wound in a holy fusion.
Some say the beard of a goat,
His stature; some mild,
Some, lecherous.

                Uncaught,
Not unbelieved, he rears within
The mythologic wood, and more
Is real the more he is unseen.
Girded in faith the varlet and the king
Silently slip inward on their dream.

ACT III: *THE UNICORN DEFENDS HIMSELF*

  . & Monoceros is an Unycorne: and a right
Cruell beast. And is not with might
Taken, hound-leap or spear-tip,
Bears not his thigh-bone white

In fear; but like Achilles' lip
Bit bloodless, drawn up
By Priam's gate, Patroclus dead,
War's cause forgotten, and the ships

That would not bear him homeward.
In hounds and kings his single sword
Shrieks like a tempest, and his tail
Is a raised scourge about their heads.

Is this what purged the pool,
What ringed by spears like spokes
Reared like a doe? (And where
Is Pentheus, the Theban fool,
Where are the Tyrrhene seamen, scales
At groin-hollow, gills at their
Earlobes?) From hounds like rocks
He strikes the blood like wine,
With wrathful tail, with crucifying horn.

ACT IV: *THE UNICORN IS CAPTURED BY THE MAIDEN*

Whereas in Africa, the old men tell,
They lure ofttimes the fierce rhinoceros
With a she-monkey on a string; who greets
His naily nose with fingers schooled
In arcane subtleties of lice and fleas.
All of a joy the wrinkled sullen beast
Turns up all fours, in a delicate frenzy.
And so the hunters come, shedding their fear,
And churn his guts to jelly with their spears.

With how much more compassion this raw maid
Awaits monoceros coyly by the pool,
Unsheathes her bosom to his holy lips
And watches where the sullen varlet creeps
Among the foliage, poising now to call.

O good Saint Venus, by your grace,
Whiter than Dian and twice as chaste,
In your lap and mercy lie,
Rapt in sensual heresy,
Half your lover, half your son,
The cuckold king, the judased unicorn.

ACT V: *THE UNICORN IS WOUNDED AND BROUGHT TO THE CASTLE*

Then tilted time unbalances us all,
Means over ends, spear-thud
And hound-yap, shoving among the leaves,
Hissing through teeth, and blood
Brighter than the bite of fear.
Not reason, death, or love can keep,
Nor kill-time tapestry encoil
The fifth-act rush and stumble of our fall.

Slain, the sword that slew, and the scourge
Scourged; five the holes wherefrom
The pure is smeared with his own blood.

The Prince is dead: long live
The King and Queen. The courtiers will not look,
And the lean hounds are uninquisitive.
Yet who is dead? for no Horatio
Howls for his friend, or clutches at the cup;
The prompter riffles through the folio,
The chittering actors hush, and in the pit
The groundlings gawk and shuffle with their feet.
For who has breathed his last, and who will come
And couplet us the end, and send us home?

EPILOGUE: *THE UNICORN IN CAPTIVITY*

And all this Francis sets before his queen:
Triumph of maid and fall of unicorn;
And in the odor of her sweetness sleeps,
For ofttimes virgins marry and princes creep
Chastened to their laps.

                 The least domestic beast,
Mateless and motherless, bends to a breast:
In Dian's ring the one-horned stag is tied
In navel-nuptial to virgin bride;
While in the chamber chastely she turns her head,
Seeing in woven dream the midnight wood,
Where, self-begotten, the kinless unicorn
Betrays himself to death to be reborn.

FROM
Simeon

COCTEAU'S OPIUM: 1

Even without any spirit of proselytizing, it is
impossible for a person who does not smoke
to live with a person who does. Each
would inhabit a different world.

Still, no one has paid much tribute to the man
who has to live *in* the addict, that madman, that poet,
that adolescent pimpled with spiritual acne;
to support him, and his wife, and his brats,
to purchase with sweat his fixes and his furniture.
Lorenzo de' Medici. Solomon Guggenheim. Pah!

And for what? But it is like trying to turn your back
on a sick cat. There is a kind of man
who cannot keep from carrying one home.

The addict, on the other hand, needs no excuse;
does he say, The world is chaos, therefore I need
my opium, my art, my ivory, my politics, my morals?
At the crucial moment, he says nothing.
He knows the world *is* order, because he knows
each scrap of chaos personally, by first name.

It is the Judas in Jesus, reason, the eternal husband,
who at the end, having paid the rent for so long,
begins to wonder if it is possible he has been forsaken.

COCTEAU'S OPIUM: 2

*The leitmotiv of de profundis. The only
crime is to be superficial. Everything which
is understood is good. The repetition of this
sentence is irritating and revealing.*

Picasso, who knows everything, will tell you:
everything is a miracle; for instance, that one
does not dissolve in one's bath "like a lump of sugar."
Everywhere, euphoria of opium, euphoria of art,
everywhere the equation of miracle with understanding,
true with beautiful, wise with good.

The miracle blasts the fig tree, from which it expects
the impossible; it demands to be understood; it has all
the significance of a man kicking a cat. It is the blind
damning the blind for not being able to conduct
a guided tour in this country of miracles. *De profundis,*
in the place of suffering, where everything is understood.

Like the noble fig, let us accept our punishment;
"a tree must suffer from the rising of its sap."
Certainly we have not been good; innocence, like ignorance,
is no excuse. Ask the adolescent, ask the addict
taking the cure, or the first weed of spring;
every morning, rising, rising, rising, ask yourself.

"MY PAINTING WILL NEVER OFFEND"

RAPHAEL

The way Beatrice does not offend, perhaps,
she chides you for your own good; the way
Circe does not offend, it is the smell
of the other pigs that assails your nostrils.

However there is always the danger of replacing
the beau ideal with the least common denominator,
the true Rheingold Girl, so inoffensive as
to be completely invisible, odorless, a Virgin.

No martyrdoms, no Last Judgments, and after one or two
youthful indiscretions, no crucifixions either;
he who had seen the streets splash in the blood
of Grifone's victims, and then in Grifone's,
preoccupied with the harmony of gestures.

Not to offend Jesus is one thing; not to offend Judas,
another. Judas has paid for his good manners
with a sensitive stomach. Everything offends him.
Something simple please, chopped steak and a baked potato.
Jesus, on the other hand, has a stomach like a boiler;
where he hangs, nothing can offend him but himself.

Yet if we could smell her out, that Lady of Silences,
who can lead men, at her whim, to heaven or hell,
resigned to be saints or satisfied to be swine;
she would bring a peace like the Son of God,
not in his aspect of Florence Nightingale, nor either
wearing Marx's whiskers over his goatee,
but as that god of women, Dionysus,
wearing nothing but an archaic smile,
and, over his article, a cluster of purple nipples.

THE SERPENT CHARMER

(AFTER JEAN LEON GÉRÔME)

This smooth stripling wears nothing but a snake,
festoons of the beast ripple along his back
and thighs; the head he holds aloft, it is
too somnolent to raise itself alone.
Gérôme has shown us all this elsewhere:
the Turkish lady who crouches at the bath;
over her head the black and harsh-clothed maid
begins to tip an urn of freezing water;
and in the market-place a buyer rubs
his hard forefinger on the slave-girl's teeth.

A violent story, beauty and the beast;
yet what a curious dryness in the telling.
Or is it meticulous love, that dotes as long
on the lovely inscrutable arabic on the wall
as on the sheikh who sprawls against it, among
his half-wild men? Yet finally, here is the source
of dryness, of beauty and beast, of love, of hate:
watching the naked boy and snake, this face
under the black tarboosh is a snarl of delight.

THE EFFECT OF THE POEM

The effect of the poem, like opium, is immediate.
The good patient downs his placebo and waits
for something; preferably negative, a cheap thrill.

But the poem, like salvation, does not come cheap.
Immediate, yes, and nothing down; the payments, however,
continue the rest of your life. For this reason

most people, like tragic heroes, would rather wait
until the last possible minute before purchasing any.

This the addict knows, and the saint, and the true
religious martyr (whom we must not confuse
with the masochist who blunders into a church),

and this the learned astronomer knows, who walks
into a manhole while tallying his stars.

THE FLAGPOLE SITTER

1

Slowly the world contracts about my ears.
First morality goes, then love, then fear
of my death; then beauty, which is bearable truth,
then truth unbearable; then pleasure, then pain.
Rocking at last in the irreducible sun,
slowly, more slow, more slow, I leave behind
even the memory that I was ever a man.

2

Like a shadow passing over the brain, from back to front,
a cool silver, a heat that looks like coolness as it runs,
molten, over the dipping ladle; this is not sleep,
but a gliding darkness, a shadow conscious of nothing
but itself, yet knowing that so intensely, it is bright.

3

When the wind blows,
a few leaves fall to the ground;
where have I been?

4

From those fat green burghers, nodding their hundred chins
at the wind's words, conspiratorial whispers,
I purchased nothing; I passed among their wares
taking nothing, wanting nothing, looking for the exit.
How did I find that city of mossy gutters?
Keeping always to my room, I was poorly prepared,
soothed by the safety of angles, the wisdom of corners
where three unruffled surfaces agree.
One moment of absence, and down the alley,
before me and behind, that army of
obscene salesmen, vegetable, complacent,
plucking at my shirt with their green fingers.

5
Seeing it, I am no longer part of it.
Part of it no longer, I forfeit the right
to be a paradigm. Forfeiting that right,
I become totally free.

6
I have begun to know the true weight of my body.
Slowly the fluid settles in my legs;
it seeps into my shoes, great blisters form,
my final illness. My rivers run into the air;
at the last, a dry leaf on a barren tree,
I shall release my hold, and be blown away.

THE FAIRY IN THE NEXT CHAIR

The fairy in the next chair is telling
his barber about Horace. (He was a
better poet, only he was so *cold*.)

Whereas the man on my hair told
me that winter was here. Outside
a cold rain is preparing to fall.

With difficulty, and probably in
some peril of shipwreck, Horace
returned to Rome. At Philippi, his

shield lay where he threw it. Praise
to Mercury, who in a mist huddled
him to safety. Outside the mist is

hardening into rain. The barber has
confided to me that he likes a drink
now and then (for the cold) but it is

bad for business. Business is bad
all over. In the next chair the
fairy is telling the man about

restraint. Outside the winter edges
the day with rain. Business is bad
all over (excess and restraint). Squat

Horatius cautions against avarice. Behold,
what infamy and ruin rise from a large
dish. Cold Flaccus remembers his shield

in Macedon, remembers the instruction of
hunger. Now my rhyming heat is cooled.
Outside the rain practices a cold restraint.

ORACLE

It is I, Orpheus, speaking through a mouthful of dust;
to hell with Apollo, I can keep still no longer.
Listen, Finkel, stop piecing me together
in your bounding iambics. Besides, you read too much;

the tune the stones will dance to is not in the books.
Inside your wife is sleeping, with fine long legs,
whom Hades has not yet noticed. While there is time,
get off your ass and make the most of her.

THE HERO

THE GARDEN

THE HERO'S MOTHER IS A ROYAL VIRGIN; HIS FATHER IS A KING.

Tuesday and Friday evenings at half-past five
regular as an alarm the doorbell rammed
my heart against my shoulder-blades. I opened,
suffered the scrape of that determined kiss;
and kissed him back. That was my end of it. Still,
lugging his coat into my mother's room,
I think I sensed his part was only the harsh
reflection of my own: to play at once
the stranger and the king in his own house.
Softly I laid that coat on my mother's bed
and turned and marched into the living room.

Sundays we drove, in good weather, out in the country,
alone among traffic, unspeaking, like fugitives,
grimly took notice of trees, sniffed at the dogwood;
spring jammed us together in a garden of shifts and clutches.
Squeezed in the vise of that silence it seemed to me
they had shared in the past, not simple knowledge, but flesh.
Like twins joined at the breast they had drunk of each other;
now must they turn to speech, merely because
someone (so they might live) had wrenched them apart?

Once, coming back, I opened the door for a flower;
a cider-jug crashed in the roadway. Wordless with choler,
for a moment he choked on something; then he hit me.
We sat there silent in the odor of ripening apples.

The Hero

EXILE IN EGYPT

AN ATTEMPT IS MADE TO KILL HIM, BUT HE IS SPIRITED AWAY,
AND REARED BY FOSTER PARENTS IN A FAR COUNTRY.

Dreams stood me in good stead, there in that country.
In the land of my affliction, nobody murmured,
'Behold, this dreamer cometh.' Safe for a time
from the pit, the knife to throat, the stealing, selling,
in a household of women slowly I perfected my weapons:
weaving, saving, tenderness, small deceit;
but weakness in special, my one true advantage.

Weakness in all forms I made work for me.
(Though not, like women, simply by brandishing;
rather, giving when pressed, conceding, admitting,
winning, shameless, by small retreats. But winning.)
Let the strong man waggle his fist, I back off rhyming;
let the wise man floor me with fact, him I confound
with the quick disarming grin of a metaphor.

Far from my father's business, a while I kept
the seven lean years at bay. And even there,
in the time of hunger, it was dreams that saved me.

LACUNA

WE ARE TOLD NOTHING OF HIS CHILDHOOD.

We are told every trifle, soon or late;
what we hear is quite another matter.
The cries of Phalaris' victims, whom he roasted
over a slow fire in a brazen bull,
fell like soft music on the tyrant's ear.

And what of the shrieking children in the street,
pressing the sheriff's quest, the outlaw's trial?
The game is music but the cries are real.

THE RETURN

ON REACHING MANHOOD HE RETURNS TO HIS FUTURE KINGDOM.

I stop at the edge of the field and he comes out running,
his face blown out; his dignity flies to the wind.
He throws his arms around me. I stand here
smelling his bad teeth, bearing no rancor.
His hands pat, pat on my back, for no words come:
I hold my little speech and wait for the moment.

He is shouting. I know that voice. When I was small
he sent me inside with it once to wash my hands.
Weeping, my hands unreal under the water,
I cried to the Lord to drown him in that basin.
When I came out he was standing by the door:
'You are not my son,' he said. 'A son would love me.
I am not wanted here.' He opened the door
and left. I know that voice. He is shouting;
already at all the windows faces appear,
the door opens, my arrival is a fact.

The women are all questions. I have a mind, almost,
to tell them where I have been, the tall trucks booming
down the night, the nights under porches, the nights
outside roadhouses, the nights inside. I have
a mind almost to tell them, but it is all right,
they will not wait for an answer: too much has happened
in the meantime to them. And suddenly in the doorway
that one last face; I raise my eyes to those
indignant eyes. The old man goes, placating,
in a voice I have not heard, but now I know it.

And how should I tell those eyes it is a mistake,
that never pleaded for a thing, or wept into water?
That I plunged my hands into a quivering face,
and the face dissolved? Can I say I have not come back?

The Hero

In the kitchen the fire flares up at the dripping calf;
I have come back. Is it worth it to tell those eyes
how the house is a different house, how that cracked voice
changes each minute from the voice I knew?

I said it there in the field, but no one listened:
I was wrong in the eyes of heaven, and in his eyes,
and though I have come back home, this is not home,
and that is not my father, nor this his son.

THE SLEEPING KINGDOM

HE MARRIES A PRINCESS AND BECOMES A KING. FOR A TIME HE
REIGNS UNEVENTFULLY.

The horses stand up again and shake themselves,
the flies stir on the wall, the fire brightens,
the maid goes on plucking the chicken, and the cook
gives such a slap to the scullery boy he yells.

For three years now it has been like that every morning;
and watching the horses wheel, the dogs in snow,
the thrill is not diminished. The wise were wrong:
you can never have too much of a good thing.

No, with a little luck, and moderate taxes,
it should keep going. Even in off years
the wine is passable; and who can kick
if the crops are plentiful and the people happy?

For a while I walked the corridors when I came.
In every room they hung like tapestries,
as if time had snagged on the nail of four o'clock,
at day's dead center, banal afternoon:

the throne-room empty but for one maid,
dusting and dusting a mantel; upstairs a guest
climbed forever into his dinner clothes;
neither the night begun nor the day ended.

And yet the dailiest gesture seemed to me,
simply by virtue of its hanging there,
translucent and inevitable and fine.
Even the dust stayed dancing in the sun

in formal patterns. I thought, And who am I
to blow like a wind behind such attitudes?
Having no use for perfection, however, they thank me.
Later in the tower, watching those little breasts

lift toward me imperceptibly, and fall,
I felt desire sprout in the dark like a tuber.
But bending my mouth to that perfect mouth I wondered
from what it was I had meant to save this kingdom.

THE HIGH PLACE

BUT LATER HE LOSES FAVOR WITH THE GODS, AND MEETS WITH A
MYSTERIOUS DEATH AT THE TOP OF A HILL.

That was a long row to hoe to reach this dung-heap,
Pangaion, Pisgah, Calvary, Parnassus;
but a wrench of the head, or the heart, one stick in the ribs,
and the bone turns music, and the flesh word.

I had a mild flame, I thought, though once in a while
it might have been, when I was singing, your voice
bouncing off the walls, your lightning at my fingers;
between those moments was a long hard time.

Down to the last wheeze and rattle, so it goes,
you come right to it, and I yell, I bleed;
here on the brink of Zion you forsake me.
Just once more, send me a sign, while I have eyes.

The Hero

APOTHEOSIS

HIS CHILDREN, IF ANY, DO NOT SUCCEED HIM. HIS BODY IS NOT
BURIED, BUT NEVERTHELESS HE HAS ONE OR MORE HOLY
SEPULCHRES.

Toward the last he began to mistrust his friends.
The sound of his own voice soothed him, he wandered about
the country giving readings. Everywhere
he scattered into the miracle-famished crowd
bright loaves and fishes, for a moderate fee.
In the morning, however, one woke with a bitter taste,
and a dozen, perhaps, of hard inedible lines.

Now in a thousand attics red-eyed boys
wrestle his dicta. All night they travel his footsteps,
in the same taverns drink the identical drink;
homeward at morning, down the same dim street,
reeling a slope of nausea into bed.
Along the wall his fables sit like stones;
he rose (one hears) to heaven from one of these.

LETTER TO AN ALTO MAN

"Any note I want to, any time."
That's what you said, I think of it often.
Knees bent, hunched over your horn,
running your fingers up and down as if
over a row of hard golden nipples.

Nothing you do is wrong: it cries with pleasure!
(Between sets we lit up in the alley,
and walked about in the night where nobody fluffs.)

You were married, the last time I heard,
had a daughter, and drove to a thousand horns
a bus in South Chicago. I have a daughter.
(The same night fingers the bumps of Chicago,
though you or I stay home.) We do what we will.

Or might as well. Nothing we do is wrong:
solid, the notes rise in the smoky air,
one after the other, of their own accord.

RUMPELSTILTSKIN

It is not possible to spin gold out of straw
you know that   I know that   but it was not so
in the old days   then people were slave
to a strange benevolent darkness   they thought
overnight   peasant girls could be turned into princesses
the King thought so   the miller thought so
even the miller's daughter thought so
she thought it was merely impossible for *her*   only
Rumpelstiltskin knew better   he knew however
that every morning   when the sun struck through the window
just so   the straw became gold as any gold
it is always given to men with ridiculous names
to keep worthless secrets like that   in a land of fools

It was this secret the new queen finally discovered
and not his name   which he did not utter simply
because it embarrassed him   once the truth was out
however   and it was clear that anybody could turn the trick
the Queen began to mock him with his name   Rumpelstiltskin
Rumpelstiltskin   she giggled   Rumpelstiltskin

BONES

We let the forsythia go one more day,
watching the shrivelled yellow duncecaps fall
in a half-circle of broken sunlight on the floor.
Like last week's leftovers; though no one will eat them,
for the crime of waste we take another whiff
before, at arm's length, we relinquish
our tenuous hold into the garbage can.

A week ago I tore two dozen switches
out of the great clump by the driveway,
careful not to disturb, like drops of water,
the dark buds perilous along their length.
We forced them. Some ring that phrase has. We tore
them where they stood and stood them naked
in a bowl, and watched them in synthetic spring
dress themselves and then undress again.
And then one more day we let them stand.

Though what a day mattered to them or us
I couldn't answer, snapping their slender backs
one by one to fit them in the garbage.
Was it the need to let the bare bones read their message
there against the pale wall like a Chinese
character for death-with-feet-in-water?
Outside much more where that came from
nods darkly still in the late winter wind.

STILL LIFE

The truth is, a man has to go out of his way
to choose three apples, a cup, and a butter-knife
for company at the bottom of love's ladder.
It would have been so much more soothing to think,
as long as one began with illusion in any case,
that he might as well live out his novitiate
watching some wench offer between two fingers
"the strawberry of her breast."
                                        Or how moral one felt
lifting again that limp form down from the tree,
whose Death was so much less dead than these
impersonal groceries, motionless on the table.
These apples will neither save nor curse;
their only virtues are, that they can be bought,
are edible till they rot, and will inform you,
if you choose to attend, that the world you move in
is round, palatable, composed, and incorrigibly itself.

SONIC BOOM

Nothing has happened, nothing has been broken,
everything is still in place, including yourself;
even now the juice of alarm begins to settle:
the bomber drags away her diminishing roar.
Nothing has happened; this was practice,
you are free to return. If there is a day
to come when you will be called out
to answer for somebody else's doings, this is not it.

Yet what is this delicate balance, that it shall not
be shaken? On the bookcase the figurine teeters;
which of its two thousand years gives it the right
to withstand one blow of the wind? Somewhere over
the plains an angel gathered enough speed
to outrun even the sound of her own voice.
In consequence, for miles around the night
exploded with the violence of her escape.
Yet she has not escaped. Behind her
and her ghostly silence, wherever she goes,
she drags like a harrow her unsettling past.

THE HUSBAND

When the man arrives tomorrow, bearing a token:
"Come, I will show you. Leave everything here;
dead weight; none of it matters," will I go?

A wife, two kids, my manuscripts, my car?
When I am eighty, and have outlived my debtors,
once more he will come. Then I'll go with him.

THE FATHER

When I am walking with the children, and a girl
still hard in the buttocks bends to them with a laugh,
my heart bangs where it hangs in my empty carcass.
But you knew that. It has already passed
the stage of neighbors' gossip and attained
the clarity of an historical fact.
A myth comes down your street: here on my right
toddles my twinkling daughter, who loves me, while
on my left marches my son, who does not.

It is all true, but it does not matter;
in twenty years my son and I will have reached
a silent understanding, whereas (poor fool,
already growing hollow) some pimply bastard
will have made off with my blessings and my daughter.

FUNERAL PROCESSION
(AFTER RENÉ CLAIR)

Motionless, the camera eye allows
them to pass: the carriage glides over
the cobbles with a few involuntary shudders;
now the mourners, a silk formality of hats;
each simulates, with varying success,
the singleminded gravity of a wheel.
Their legs cause them a little difficulty,
also their children. The camera begins to peruse,
from carriage to mourners, and from mourners to carriage;
approaching, receding; now the carriage arrives;
or the mourners retreat. What have we seen?

Before we are certain, something imperceptible happens:
the mourners are walking with a new determination;
in the carriage some pressure is at work, it surges
toward the edge of the screen. Look: they rise up
on their toes, as if rebounding; the cobbles become
a sea of rubber balls; they leap, they dance.
The carriage is performing a series of jetés.

The cameraman tightens an invisible spring:
the mourners twitch like electrocuted frogs,
in their legs the strain of delight is beginning to tell,
one or two seem intent on reaching the carriage;
a rumor has gone out that the coffin is loose.
But the mourners will have none of it, they are running.

They manage to keep up. This new assurance
repays them for the loss of their dignity;
with élan, if with grace no longer, they enter the spirit
of the chase: at last they have found their part.

The ground has blurred to air; the great black kite
buffets on the wind, rises; the mourners trail,
a fluttering departure of rags and crepe.

54

MARRIAGE

The arrangement is essentially comic,
silent, and familiar to the audience:
you walk, and then I, six feet behind.
We are carrying something between us,
not visible, but obvious enough.

We are careful, though not beyond reason;
we do this every day. The audience
knows what to expect: the hero comes,
intent on his labors, of which we have
no part. Whatever he is doing,
we are only here to make things difficult;
that is, to go on doing what we are doing,
being careful, but not beyond reason.

You pass; always the gentleman, he waits.
Between you and me the distance is endless;
the audience catches its breath. Now.
Flattened against the glass his handsome
empty face registers the first flicker of surprise.

I pass. He will continue his labors;
he will return, presently, bearing
for the heroine a cluster of wilted flowers.
We go on. The audience no longer notices
that we continue to bear between us
something invisible, difficult to manage,
fragile, and slightly besmeared.

BELMONTE

1

Had he Joselito's frame, he would have desired
nothing better than to conduct the sacrifice
with the same calm and purity of motion.

Called to his task, not born, hampered by doubts,
and a fine sense of his imperfections, he sought
new arrangements, new laws, a modern art.

Knowing the ritual must be at all costs preserved,
or man suffer the loss of his link with death,
he bade the priest assume the place of the bull.

As the bull leaned to the sword, he would lean to the horns,
proffering the secrets of his groin and breast;
he became the torero of three olés and an *ay!*

2

And what was it for the mob at the pyramid's foot
that the pampered hero, calm in his vegetable potions,
delivered up his heart to the ragged blade?

What was he worth, aloft, disdainful, withdrawn?
Yet they left released, as if from actual chains,
from the guilt which men call pity, from fear of death,

in the exhausted bliss that follows the creative act;
in that Sunday torpor they filed to their apartments;
for these he was victim, and not the stone-faced priests.

RIMBAUD

after the violence and visions, true smoker, sinks
into a world of his own, of shadows sharp
as knives, of strangers, and no use writing home,
having lost the language.

I speak of Rimbaud,
that sharp professor's baby, that shibboleth.
And still the punks complain: Why can't you shout,
'Oh, palms! Oh, garbage cans! Oh,
how I love my baby!' And I sink in my chair, wondering,
What other language can I speak? Rimbaud
is a word I know. I speak him. Is he less than a palm?

Among the racket and flies he walks, oh, palms!
oh, lovely kootch dancer in the drinking-tent!
Does he see nothing? Have his eyes been clouded by time?
Is he suddenly no longer the stranger? In the dark
pocket of his sex he watches the girl, offering,
thrusting, opening, closing. And does not speak.

MIDAS

Dying of his secret, he crept to the water's edge
on hands and knees. All night he dreamed, giddy
among the rushes, an ass swayed in the wind
twitching his ears. All night he heard the whisper
of lovers' thighs, and the grey rasp of the dead.
At the first glimmer of morning he thrust out his neck;
the cries pumped out of his blackness like rusted laughter.

Later, having thought better of it, sitting
in the great hall full of suppliants, he heard
someone whistle out in the yard the ass's lament.
The stream was clearer now, it purled out
into the sun, it leapt, it ran down the windows;
the curtains gleamed like cloth of gold. Soon
Midas himself was humming it. It was really quite catchy.

OEDIPUS AT SAN FRANCISCO

He left me exposed on a hill of woman, my mother.
I paid him back at every crossroads, quitting
school, smoking pot, writing poems
he couldn't fathom; after a while it palled.
The past is dead now, neither of us could care less.

But mamma, that's something else; no peace with *her*.
You can't turn your back, she is everywhere, under
your feet, like the ground. The old man's prod withdrawn,
she turns slowly inanimate; every year
she gets harder and harder to push away. It isn't
enough, any more, that she rarely calls. She is there;
and there's no getting around it, I am a bastard.

LETTING GO

To be on the wire is life; the rest is waiting.
KARL WALLENDA

One lets go of the platform, not the wire;
the walk is life. The times between are only
a kind of waking sleep, a death-in-life.

True, death is always there, night lady, lover
(grace of the bull-maid tumbling over the horns;
the numb ascent of the addict, out of life;
the dying backward of the poet into childhood,
walking the line half-drunk and mesmerized).

From the other platform, now, she comes, she glitters,
though under the lights no one can see her but you.
Both of you may as well fall now, as later:
back on the ground you will flush, as in shame, and bow.

A Joyful Noise

LOVE SONG FOR AN AVOCADO PLANT

Once maybe, a man could marry a plant.
Nowadays, though he bow and sprinkle before one,
the rites and prayers have lost their ancient sense:
he goes about the business like a plumber.

How tall she was, and fecund, how heavy with fruit,
though the taste of paradisal flesh is faint
on a dusty tongue.
                    (Except for the chirimoya,
which smells faintly of puke: ghost-puke: angel-puke:
the holy original bitch was revolted by nothing.)

And still she deigns to blossom in this province
of variable weather, fall, and dust.
(How pale so far from paradise, and faint!)
I prod the soil at her feet, as if she might,
for all my shy caressing, rise with me.

In the country of the dead, the leper is queen:
I bring her drink, I brush the dust from her shoulders;
the two of us quake in the thin December sun.

CHIMP

Stan Laurel. It's when he scratches his head;
rueful, a little vague, but definitely
a thinking animal. (The same unmixed appeal,
like children and the very old.) Why is it
so reassuring that man is not the first
two-legged beast to discover he thinks, and with what?

Left to his own devices, he travels alone,
or in twos, or threes;
not, like his more categorical brothers,
in orders, complete with vows and hierarchies.
Think how our early fathers, more often than not,
were surly anchorites. No company
would have them.

(Some barefaced son of a slightly dubious mother
scratches his skull, and finds
the fly still walking upside-down inside.
The motels blink their neon-yellow eyes,
Fords growl in the underbrush: the jungle
is safe again for democracy and the legion.)

He looks at me from under his rueful wrinkle;
I am less reassured.
I want to whisper: I am not with the others.
Essential man is alone, whether caged or free,
whether nose to tail with his mate in the bog of Desire,
or trailed by a half dozen wet-nosed consequences.

Through the hand-polished bars he hears it the way it comes out:
I am not your keeper.

PLANH

*... The simple imaginative mind may have
its reward in the repetition of its own silent
working coming continually on the spirit
with a fine suddenness ...
O for a life of sensations rather than of
thoughts!* KEATS, *Letters*

It's the same old song in the ancient tongue
(whether the table remembers the Word or not),
the same old reliable bedtime story:
the hero, the virgin, the hill, the spear in the gut,
four tales sung to a single tune.
It's the bonny prince in the tower and the warden's daughter,
the haunted sword and the wandering wounded knight,
one tale sung to the four old tunes,
one thief nailed by a band of virgins,
one spear and four terrible wounds.

Four songs for the lord and his noisy table
(blind drunk, fighting drunk, or out),
four tales to the same terrible end:
the man, the maid, the mountain, the pain in the gut;
that last sweet ordeal, when the walls come down,
when the nerves like easy women in every street
tangle in their arms the gaunt invader,
man and maid and mountain rolled into one.

Like the last thrust of love, when the banging blood
stops dead, and you catch, in the same old dark,
your own thump and whisper in your ear,
two hearts drum to a single tune;
the song buries his bright head in your belly,
one shaft in one terrible wound.

THE DYSPEPTIC FLORIST

I

When I was young and sixty,
before I got the business,
I walked about the city
with flowers in my arms,
and nobody saw me.

Plainclothesman, robber, spy,
the smiling bolshevik,
a leathery messenger boy
with wings on his overshoes;
I like to think as I passed
they felt a breeze.

She lived in a street by day,
a carnival by night,
over a coffee-house,
up one narrow flight,
knock at the farthest door
painted toenail pink;
she opened up the color
and tipped me a wink.

She was breasts all over,
like the Babylonian whore;
her voice, of course,
was like a scratch on brass.
Black roses I remember
bloomed on my chest like hair.
A leathery messenger
gets in anywhere.

Later in the kitchen
she warmed my blood
with instant coffee:
Doctors! she crowed,

The Dyspeptic Florist

Pay no attention.
Can the body die?
Can the wrinkle hide
the bone inside?

Seven years I sat in the window
turning brown at the edges.
I have it straight from the flowers;
they are too simple to lie,
they are too pretty to stoop
to ambush and deceit.
Listen to what they say;
they speak to me from the root,
they drop their little secrets
at my feet:
How can the body die?
Even our dust is fragrant.

2

There is no bottom to failure,
the opportunities in that direction
are limitless.

I never believed in anything hard enough
to hurt me if I hit it.
Death is, after all, a relative thing.

Is Shakespeare dead? or Hitler?
Is Oedipus?
Till the world goes poo! you can go on being a loser.

The Dyspeptic Florist

3

When the old man called me to his house, dying of roses,
and laid his debts and blessings on my head,
he called it business.

He loved me like a son, he said
(some son,
a sixty-year-old boy in a messenger hat).

Business is business, honey, you give and you get,
you eat and you get eaten.
Seven lean years I ate nothing but roses.

I dieted down to a whisper;
all they found was dust on the elephant ears.
Somebody else should have the business.

4

So look out your window, go,
dump your stale gardenias
on boys in sharp blue suits and their pin-curled Annies.

Squint at their titties and rattle your bright-green paper.
One day the roses will wake up and scratch out your eyes,
one day the gardenias will sit up in bed,
whiter than schoolgirls, and drown you in their sick-sweet breath.
One rainy Monday even the nicest children
turn and kick the old man down the stairs.

Wait,
they'll get you, the flowers:
they'll sit on your grave.

THE IMPOSTOR

I am the original Cat-of-nine-lives,
excuse the glove;
doppelgänger to the man with seven wives,
who was too busy wifing it up in St. Ives
to come and explain.
I am doppelgänger to any man with a life
or a wife
high, wide and handsome enough to hold me.
I fly my own plane.

I may show up in Milwaukee at any hour:
Remember St. Ives!
May their god have mercy on the men of Milwaukee
and their wives.

It's one life or the other;
the same five flying senses,
same heart, same liver,
same tongue, sweetbreads, gizzard,
clatter-and-wheezing,
past rhyme, past reason,
one span of springs and winters to listen
to what the pieces are saying to each other.

If the lights go out, we'll fly by candle-light,
if the elm-trees die, we'll bang behind the billboards:
May the god of the mills have mercy tomorrow
on the men of Chicago.

HANDS

The poem makes truth a little more disturbing,
like a good bra, lifts it and holds it out
in both hands. (In some of the flashier stores
there's a model with the hands stitched on, in red or black.)

Lately the world you wed, for want of such hands,
sags in the bed beside you like a tired wife.
For want of such hands, the face of the moon is bored,
the tree does not stretch and yearn, nor the groin tighten.

Devious or frank, in any case,
the poem is calculated to arouse.
Lean back and let its hands play freely on you:
there comes a moment, lifted and aroused,
when the two of you are equally beautiful.

REFLECTIONS ON VIOLENCE

All things are full of holes,
the difference between open and closed is a matter of degree.
To the point of diminishing returns,
the finer the nozzle the further the spray.
You have only to open one door of a burning theater
to let people out.

I have seen fear burning in the tail-lights of the halted cars,
red through the acrid black;
my nostrils flared at the scent of catastrophe.
The theater continued its convulsions, vomiting now and then
a man or a child.

I have seen a fire hose turned on a man in a doorway,
but only in a photograph;
the pressure of anguish which drove the man and the water,
held at the same pitch, one against the other, forever.
In the morning, something still hung in the thin white air;
it was like smelling a photograph of catastrophe.

I remember the fireman lifting his rod of water
to bless the theater's burning hair;
and out of the stony mouth, swaddled in smoke,
a child emerging forever.

A JOYFUL NOISE

Let each man first seek out his proper totem;
let each man come in his turn, with his cross and his treasure,
let him cleave to his wife, or his enemy, or his car,
let him praise the holy fool who first introduced them;
for whom Christopher has joined together, let no man sunder,
for he has packed us cheek to cheek like tiles on a bathroom floor,
Job by his worm, Balaam by his ass, our scrubbed and gleaming
    faces turned toward heaven.

Let Christopher praise with a cat,
for it sits on idols;
let Jeoffry praise with Christopher, poor Christopher!
for he loved his prank, nor spat without provocation, and the rat
    has bit him;
let Samuel Johnson pray in the street with a tambourine.

Let Gogol pray with his nose,
let Van Gogh pray with an ear,
let Poe praise with his liver,
let Pound praise with a curse,
let Blake praise with a handful of dust in our faces,
let Finkel praise with ashes, for his fire is out.

Let Finkel's wife bless patiently with Finkel,
for a high little star provoketh wonder;
let Finkel's children bless with the best they can get;
let all men's children bless,
let them choke the streets, and the balconies, and the squares,
for the churches will be packed, no room for kneeling;
let them fill their lungs as they can, under the circumstances,
let them all begin to holler at once, according to their custom, like
    one vast apocalyptic Recess,
let each one and his brother turn up his scrubbed, gleaming face
    to the sun, and yell.

A POEM AND A PRAYER TO ST. HOFFSTEIN

St. H was born at the age of thirty-three
to an elderly candy-store in the West Bronx;
he set up shop at once in a room in the back:
one iron cot, a box of books, and Madam
Blavatsky.
The iron-faced virgin glared on his every breath
from the lintel, with a thumbtack in her forehead.
St. H endured terrible migraine headaches.
So passed his childhood.

At the age of thirty-three (looking twelve years older),
blinking behind his glasses his brown good-natured
eyes of an intelligent cocker spaniel,
St. H stepped out of his shell into the sunlight.
An angular secondhand bookstore from Queens
played stoop-ball with her runny-nosed kid brother:
the scene was etched in sunlight,
the dust glittered.

St. H performed several middle-aged miracles.
He buried a half dollar at the foot of a gingko
in front of his mother's, the next day dug up a dime.
He ate no meat, saying, A man Is what he Eats.
I am a Vegetable.
He drank water as if it were wine.
He made old women smile.
For weeks on end he lived on absolutely nothing
but an occasional slice of love on a dry bagel,
simply because he forgot.

He wrote a book on The Squaring of the Circle,
proposing therein a new geometry;
Theorem One: A line is beautiful.
He lectured on Dreams at the Lonely Hearts Club social.

All day Sunday he stood in front of the Museum
of Natural History, waiting for Martians.

They walk among us, he said when we were assembled.
They wear our clothes and our faces and speak our language.
Somebody asked the obvious. He smiled:
They will recognize *me*.

St. H, patron of all those
who are born middle-aged, with a Ph.D. in Astrology,
of all those the Martians have forgotten,
St. H of the Lonely Heart,
St. H of the Square,
St. H of Queens, Shrine-in-back-of-the-bookstore
(she has gone blowsy, the children all have colds,
a constant haggle over the vegetables),
Gentle Spaniel:
I lift your homely image with outstretched hands,
I drive from this room the demons of Pride and Impatience.

St. H, may I be thirty-three forever,
like you.

ONE

I sat under the tree
and would not love or die.
One out of many is one.
Only the dying know
how to take it with you,
only the dying of love
eat, have, give.
Nothing from none is none.

Neither abed nor dead,
leaning against my tree,
neither one nor none
I slept precariously
under the stern, sad
eyes of the moon and sun.

TWO

Until I gave you all
you were half-beautiful.

Until I cast off thought
you had but half a wit.

And still I am a fool,
nor are you beautiful.

For I lost my lovely part
to consummate your wit.

For you cast off your mind
that I might not go blind.

THREE

Before I came, the house was empty.
Half-hearted ghosts moaned in the bedroom
or trailed in their sheets,
but nobody saw them or heard them.
No one left in the morning or came home at night.
No one ate in the dining room.

Nothing is one and one,
nothing and nothing is three,
everything under the sun
was born with me.

I filled the night with my voice,
and you were created.
I wake up the dust and the sunlight every morning.
I will jump up and run yelling after the seasons,
and skin my knees, and cry out.
I will cry out arrival and departure.
I will shriek excellent reason after reason
for going and for coming.

Three into three is one,
one into three is three,
you shall be whole again:
listen to me.

COUPLETS

The poem is the eye of an angel looking over its shoulder
at its wife, its children, and its car.

If you look a poem in the eye you will see yourself.
Think: What is the angel looking at?

In the poem's room, both the windows are mirrors,
the mirror is clear as a window.

When the poem looks in the mirror it sees
another poem looking back.

No water is still
as the water that lies asleep on the poem's wall.

An angel looks out of it, radiant
with what it sees in the room.

The poem, naked, hides its guilty secret
with long beautiful hands.

When you walk through the wall it may be difficult
but not for long.

When you kiss, remember to look through its eyes
into the water.

It will be like kissing the wind, or burning crystal,
or yourself.

It will be like wrestling a river, a tree, a wife,
for life.

THE CROSS-EYED LOVER

For C

1

I have a friend, she says.
I watch the silver minnow
swimming in the shadow
that flows between her breasts,
caught on a silver string.
There is a smile on her face,
I know without looking.

2

Homer went blind,
Milton went blind, looking,
Justice went blind, looking too long at Reason;
Van Gogh sent the Muse
his ear, as a token,
if only he could keep on looking.
(She hung the sun between
her burning yellow breasts;
fried to a golden brown
the brain behind his eyes,
bright blue to the end
and clear as glass.)

3

Cupid tied the bandage on himself.
Under a layer of linen
a forty-six-year-old beautician from De-troit
offers just as sweet a
target as Brigitte.
Only hanged men and little kids
learn quickly enough how not to look through it.

4
I have a friend myself.
All day he peers at naked wenches
sprawling on red velvet couches
or artificial grass,
upside-down on five-by-seven inches
of ground glass.
He says it is an art. (I have an art myself.)

5
Fuad the fakir stares at the sun all day,
all day he turns his whiskered puss to the sun;
he knows damned well his eyes
were burned out years ago.
And what do you think he does
after the sun goes down?
Wouldn't you give your shell-like ear to know.

6
My friend Fuad.
My pal Milton.
Meet my wife, the Muse.
(A silver mermaid leaps between her breasts;
I know without looking.)
Only a brassière salesman in his blue suède shoes
could look on her face, long,
and not go blind.

THREE FOR ROBERT RAUSCHENBERG

ONE: THE WHITE PAINTINGS

> *I always thought of the white paintings as*
> *being not passive but very—well,*
> *hypersensitive.*

1
Erase a de Kooning, to see
if there remain on the paper
traces of sanctification.
What do you sanctify next?
After the first taste of pork on your innocent finger,
there is no rest.

You will eat crawling cheese,
you will drink enough to be ill,
you will coat your mouth with cayenne,
you will stick needles between your fingers until
you can't hold onto your horn.
You will live to learn.

2
We call the fool divine
who first discovered wine.
Like Leda he knew
exactly what to do
in case of assault by a swan:
hang on.

3
And we honor the first man to be gored by a bull
to see if there would be anything beautiful
left on the sand.

Three for Robert Rauschenberg

He wasn't let into Olympus for nothing.
Like Pasiphaë
he knew what he was doing.

We set up for him in the Plaza de México
before every performance
a Coca-Cola bottle ten feet tall.

4
There is something in this that reeks of the Eternal Feminine:
this cool, hypersensitive white, like dawn
with only a few uncertain stars,
this maidenly submission to the Muse, like a temple virgin.

Assaulted daily by the god who came disguised as a stranger,
the painter turns from being man to being human,
a tourist on whatever continent, in whatever café,
talking about nothing but painting and hanging on.

5
Mother is sorry for what She did
the day the galloping ghost was laid;
Junior bellows in his bed,
Father's taken a powder.

Mother is sorry for what She hath made
in a whimsical instant She almost enjoyed;
Mother regrets having made Father mad
at the sight of Her glistening udder.

The moment was magic, bully and maid
played out the ancient rite and said
whatever they say when the ghost is laid
and the maid turns into Mother.

Mother is sorry She made the Bed,
it never did her any good,
he flew away before She could;
and so did Junior.

6
To paint a picture that has "the dignity
of not calling attention to itself":
it is to stand for hours on end in the rain
like a pool of water, thinking of nothing but painting;
no mean accomplishment for a natural man.

I try to imagine the poem aspiring to the humility
of prose, the poem saintly enough to be content
to call attention to something beyond himself;
I contemplate the word holy enough
to hide his light under a trademark; to say, Coca-Cola,
to himself, in a natural voice, over and over and over.

7
The gospel according to Satchmo, second verse
(same as the first): If you got to ask the question,
baby, you *never* going to understand the answer.

TWO: A COLLAGE

> *I'd really like to think that the artist could
> be just another kind of material in the
> picture.*

I
And it came to pass after these things, that God did tempt
    Abraham,
and said unto him, Abraham: and he said, Behold, here I am.
And Isaac spake unto Abraham his father, and said, My father:
and he said, Here am I, my son. And the Angel of the Lord
called unto him out of heaven, and said, Abraham, Abraham:
and he said, Here am I.

Three for Robert Rauschenberg

                         To keep from blinding us,
the angel Goat has consented to wear a rubber tire.

And Isaac called his eldest son, and said, my son:
and he said unto him, Behold, here am I. And Jacob likewise,
when he came: Here am I.

                         For the angel Goat
has only a single line; but he says it like a trouper.

2

There are times when it is hard, even for a saint,
to look his best; but the eyes of the angel Goat
are as clear, brown, and unambiguous
as Dad's Old-Fashioned Rimless Root-Beer Glasses.
He stands there challenging anyone in the room
with a secret smile on his battered, peaceful face.

But the angel Goodyear is a match for the angel Goat.
Clumsy out of his natural element,
nevertheless he manages to hang on
by virtue of heroic insolence and sheer dead weight,
like an albatross.

3

Ladies and Gentlemen: the Black Angel (in white)
grapples the Angel X (also in white,
a bathrobe of Genuine Angora, which he refuses to part with);
the Ultimate Mixed Match, the Card of the Century.
And the cops and the Legion of Decency helpless
to cut it out.

4

Angels, according to St. Maria-Rilke, are true
hermaphrodites: when any two get together,
the result is invariably ring-straked and peculiar;
but milder, much milder, and wilder.

5

For those who read, and those who don't, a sign:
the initial Let-there-be and the initial There-was,
interlocking; capital Cancer encircled by capital Worm
(Ourobouros of the Elephant's Graveyard, where mile on mile
the Buicks squat, like fat bisexual dowagers,
dying quietly on their knuckles, from the inside out).
For every man is a minotaur to his mother.
"All I see when I look is minotaurs," says jolly
St. Bruegel-Diego. "And minotaurs is what I paint."
The Muse must teach us this, or nothing more.
For the minotaur is Something in his kidskin shoes
and his Genuine Albatross cravat.
For the Man and his Mark are one and everywhere,
like signatures on trees, wherever flesh
has left its loving mark on living flesh;
a mutilation I wear, and all my kind,
wherever they are, and whatever they touch.
For every man is a minotaur to his mother.

6

And when I lifted up my eyes, behold, Esau came.
And Esau ran to meet me, and embraced me
like a rubber tire, and fell upon my neck,
and we wept.

THREE: THE ERASED DE KOONING

> *Look at that, the birds have freed the stop
> signs.*

I

I could easily enough have left my mark on the archduke's tunic.
I could be looking right now, if I chose, from some high window
on the whole tragic procession, through a sniper's scope.
I choose instead to leave the outline of my left hand on the wall,
blowing earth-red powder on bear grease through a hollow bone.
As Leonardo said, you either destroy, like the sculptor,

or you create. And they tell of a prince who hacked away the Jews,
seeking under the rubble a boy as hard, cold, naked and blond
as marble. He found, instead, a cocky little angel
peeing in a fountain.

                Who am I to speak? When I take away
my hand, there will be nothing there, either;
five greasy fingers full of nothing,
glinting darkly out of the earth-red ground.

2

For the fountain filleth up and brimmeth over with angel-pee,
and there is not one who thrusts his horn in the pool,
now the unicorn is gone, that does not bring up
something ring-straked and congenitally wretched.

The prince relenteth, he calleth upon the rabbi's greasy caftan
in his extremity, and the rabbi cometh. He bringeth into the room
a clod with a face like mauled granite, who creaks when he walks
like a dying oak in a storm.
                Back in her room,
the rabbi's virgin daughter moos at the general's
monogrammed black silk underwear. She will bear in time
a long-faced lout with horns and an unnatural appetite
for little girls and boys.

3

The sky is a great blue bathtub running over,
nobody left up there to fix the leak;
but, knee- or neck-deep in it, cool in the sewer,
nobody down here seems to mind in the least.

Three for Robert Rauschenberg

From where I sit, I can see down five
dripping tunnels in the stone, but not far.
At the confluence of five greasy rivers,
where all things lost or expendable collect,
I sit in the hollow of a hand that does not exist:
my sky is five blue holes in a manhole cover,
and a toad's-eye view of the muddy underwear of Buicks.

4
I put my cheek to the stock and my eye to the glass:
there is nothing on the dull-black stage but a pool of light
into which the Man of the Moment is just now gliding.

The muscles of the mind and trigger finger contract like sphincters:
through the hole in the archduke's shirt you can read history.

The plug is out, three million lives go down with a sucking sound;
but the faucet still leaks, the cocky angel is not through yet,
nor has the rabbi's daughter relinquished her taste for pork.

Mother, turn the hourglass, put another egg in the pot;
Junior shot a hole in the floor, and time is running out.

5
The angel layeth it on, and the angel eraseth,
yet the corpse sinks down between the cobblestones
not one whit faster than before, or slower;
the lovers go on taking out and putting in.

I sit in the palm of his hand, as the stone in the water;
I exult like a worm in the rain, or dust in the sunlight,
painting a pregnant smile or a black moustache
on the rosy lips of the rabbi's ambiguous daughter.

The Garbage Wars

A FEW POINTERS

Above all, the road must not be too carefully chosen.

Best, walk backwards, but map it as you go.

In the heart of the city a man circles endlessly, chamber after chamber, hands moiling behind his back, eyes locked on his shoes. He is already miles ahead of you.

Be sure when you leave to take everything with you, the table, the books, chair, the carpet under your feet. They are hard to replace. The packing will cost you some days, it is worth the expense.

Consider, at last you stand in a room much like this. Outside the air is thick with the twitter of outlandish birds, the insolent hills stare in at you through the window. You will be glad, then, to be lapped round by old newspapers.

You will be issued on arrival a wire cage. Set it in the grass, fill it with the papers, start it burning. The smoke, the velvet flakes that drift through the apertures, will cause you to weep. It will be for a moment as if you never left the city.

There will remain behind an eight foot circle of scorched grass. You will feel it for days, every anguished blade. Henceforth, take all your papers to the dump.

The receptacle may be left, however, where it is. It may be used, when the grass returns, as a cage for dandelions.

Wait. Others are on the way.

THE MAN WITH SHORT MEMORY

The man with short memory walks
into the toolshed   behind his house
gropes for the string in the dark and
kicks over the chair

                    a thread
when he catches it he is already
in the act of falling   a dangling straw
parts so easily   the ceiling flares
the shadowy rafters   reel overhead.

The man with short memory gets to his
feet   ponders the chair, fallen
he has already forgotten what he
came for, etc.

               once more he
disposes his corpse   an absent gesture
among the litter   but it is too late
in the house   the wife of the man with
short memory   sits down to dinner
with the children   his hound lies sleeping
under his chair.

THE DOG IS SICK

It suits his bowlegs and his mournful ears
to let his supper ooze onto the floor
from his untroubled throat   what has he to hide
has food become so precious he can find
no other sustenance till breakfast?

He settles comfortably in his element
yet there must be times he aches   I do
to be a cat   walks like a cat where
I can't see him   swings his ass and
leaps like a cat   stretches out in the window
and tries to purr.

WALKING THE DOG

1

I give him his head   but he can't leave
well enough   he makes his way like
the shy hand of a determined lover   strains
after sweeter liberties
                  I stiffen
the chain goes suddenly taut   I feel
the length of my arm   the blow on his throat.

2

I cast him into the wind   a dark lure
twitching in the current   he snags
on a sunken thorn   chain-snap
the cloudy sky sways overhead like frog spawn
I ride downstream   tugging impatiently.

3

The chain   a woman's invention
so cunningly linked   my fist to his throat
we're bound to each other   two halves
of a metaphor
               we wade through the wind
as through spider threads   my nerves
whicker under their sly caress
                  we drift on
trailing moony filaments   a blind man drawn
by a blind dog   into enemy country.

4

I wind the chain round my fist till it rides
mailed like a templar   between his shoulderblades
home stretch   we're neck and neck
it's hard to know who leads   and who's led
in the porchlight our shadows   unreel behind us
like distance   like speed
               we sail past our door
feet barely scraping the ground   two ghost-dry leaves
on the thin October wind.

THE GARBAGE WARS

And he dwelleth in desolate cities,
and in houses which no man inhabiteth,
which are ready to become heaps.

The
prison is
the world
of sight,
the light
of the fire
is the
sun.

The city wears about her neck a
garland of dead rats   like an
albatross   where can we stow it?
foul conglomerate   the poor, whom
charity corrupts   brain-damaged
infants marked for the heap by
starvation   the jails filled
to overflowing with the young, the
drunken and the meek   for walking
on the grass   for smoking it
for stealing cars   for lying
in front of them   snipers and
pacifists

headless dolls, bicycles without wheels,
torn cushions vomiting kapok, non-returnable bottles

(from the alleys of history step
the garbage men   an army of dog-catchers
and exterminators   marching on the ghetto
armed with headache balls and sledges)

as an example the General nails
a nation to the stake   sets it
aflame   friend and foe alike
assist via satellite   they get the
message   plain as a head on a pike
dapper little man   glaring through
gunmetal glasses   into the heart of the flame
a silk scarf blooms like a lily at his throat.

93

The Garbage Wars

The Greeks
set back-
fires to
save their
ships.

They've thrown a wall round the ghetto
withdrawn behind it   the Governor's
doubled the guard   O happy complicity!
on the hill the students have taken
the library   overturn ceremoniously
files for the letters A through E
one thousand billy-swinging fathers
burst through the doors   thunder
of tumbling books   catcalls in the ashes.

*And the fish that was in the river died; and the river
stank, and the Egyptians could not drink of the water
of the river; and there was blood throughout all the land
of Egypt.*

Did Hera-
kleitos
teach a
general
conflagra-
tion?

And the General   time's ultimate
garbage man   moves in to clean up
he rakes the streets with fire
wipes out the snipers' nests

(for the purpose at every corner great
municipal incinerators   and the smoke
thereof   and the ashes likewise
consumed   and the residue pressed
into bricks with which to build
new incinerators)

in the ghetto
the inmates have set fire to their mattresses
black clouds of acrimonious smoke
appall the suburbs

the city
thrashes in her agony   the supermarket
shrieks through her broken teeth   ten thousand
bedrooms lift their burning eyes to the constellations
for a sign.

REMARKABLE LIGHT EFFECTS   *A Dialogue with Heraclitus*

On the morning of 16 July the Chicago newspapers carried an item telling of the explosion of a munitions dump in New Mexico with remarkable light effects.

ARTHUR HOLLY COMPTON

This American system of ours...gives to each and every one of us a great opportunity if we would only seize it with both hands and make the most of it.   AL CAPONE

All my life I felt fear, but I did not know of what.

ADOLF EICHMANN

Half of it is earth and half of it is prester.   HERACLITUS

Allegiance requires a cause; a cause requires an enemy. This much is obvious

and the desired objective is not that my opponent should lie dead but that he should be soundly thrashed and humbly accept my physical and, if I am to be considered as good as a baboon, my mental superiority.

HERACLITUS: *Swine wash in the mire, and barnyard fowls in dust.*

The attacks that have since the time of Samuel's criticism of King Saul been leveled against military expenditures as waste may well have concealed or misunderstood the point that some kinds of waste may have a larger social utility

war, and only war, solves the problem of inventory.

HERACLITUS: *Corpses are more fit to be cast out than dung.*

"You are charged with the unlawful possession of two revolvers," Kapp began.
    "And two poems," Jones interrupted.

PLEASE

DONT

ARRIVE HERE

BEFORE YOUR

TIME

95

HERACLITUS: *Time is a child playing draughts, the kingly power is a child's.*

Men and women were accordingly in the streets, going about their normal business.

> The old Doctor tried to get away. Good did the shooting while I called the shots. The first two missed. At the third I called "Distance!" At the fourth the old Doctor collapsed. The weapons we used were sixteen-shot Henry repeaters, a new weapon at the time

what Masuo Kato calls 'a kind of euthanasia—a merciful release.'

HERACLITUS: *Every beast is driven to pasture with blows.*

> "In the name of the People of the State of California..." he ordered them to disperse.
> "We ARE the people! We ARE the people!" the crowd cried back.

> Unruh stopped firing and answered, "Hello."
> "This Howard?"
> "Yes...."
> "Why are you kiling people?"
> "I don't know. I can't answer that yet. I'll have to talk to you later. I'm too busy now."

The reaction is self-sustaining. The curve is exponential.

HERACLITUS: *But it was ever, and ever shall be an ever-living Fire, with measures of it kindling, and measures going out.*

The rattle of the counters died down to an occasional click. I imagine that I can still hear the sigh of relief from the suicide squad.

> The experiment had worked precisely as expected. The theoretical calculations were confirmed, and that was that.

A little cheer went up.

We were given the final proof that war is death.

> **Int.** heigh-ho! alas! alack! O dear! ah —,
> woe is me! lackadaisy! well —, lack —,
> alack— a day! well-a-way! alas the day!
> *O tempora! O mores!* what a pity! *misera-*
> *bile dictu!* O lud lud! too true!

HERACLITUS: *All the things we see when awake are death, even as all*
we see in slumber are sleep.

It was the next day before the full extent of the damage was known.

> But was there any alternative? If the General Electric
> Company did not develop the fluorescent lamp, would
> not Westinghouse?

> OUR WAY IN THE DARK—so you
> umble or fall. Life-like hands held
> eaceful prayer—glow from within
> a warm light. Special G.E. bulb
> year—night and day—for only
> teed to last 20,000 hours! Un-
> poly, 5″ high. Cord incl.
> aying Hands Night Light.   1.98

HERACLITUS: *So we must follow the common, yet though my Word is*
common, the many live as if they had a wisdom of their
own.

I hear again the voice of the Japanese reporter: 'Had it not been for
the bomb I would not be here to ask you the question.'

> **Phr.** tears —standing in, — starting from—
> the eyes; eyes —suffused, — swimming, —
> brimming —, overflowing— with tears.

HERACLITUS: *And it is law, too, to obey the counsel of one.*

THAW

Don't try to jump over your own shadow.   GYPSY PROVERB

Nails snapped in the boards all night
dog whimpered under the reeling wagon
yet this afternoon   the garbage
that lay so long by the door like
many-colored stone
                                        begins to rot.

Tomorrow we'll strip from the windows
all straw and tarpaper   all blankets
boards   torn overcoats   and burn them
in the first untrammelled fire
of the new season.

GENTLY

Last fleck of snow   cupped
in the dead grass like alien sugar
I take the day by the throat   gently
as not to bruise it   carry it
back to my cave   to light the way down.

98

LOVE SONG

Compassionate muse
indulgent muse
constant
cool
intransmutable
tranquil
grave

classical muse
chaste
felicitous
elegant
ardent muse
exigent muse
wilful
uncompromising

why
have I waited
so long
to mention this?

GESTURE

My arm sweeps down
   a pliant arc
      whatever I am
         streams through my
           negligent wrist:
the poem
      uncoils
         like a
            whip, and
snaps
softly   an inch from your enchanted face.

TIME OUT

My mind shrugs off his threadbare winter poems
stone broke   hands in his pockets
he stalks the freeway   not a thought to his name
whistling
             April slides her long cool fingers
under his shirt.

BREATHER

The yearling crops at the fence post
a crown of burrs   in his forelock
the aspens twitch their sequinned buttocks
in the afternoon light   still I can't
touch
             across my shuddering brow
one black word crawls   it's time I
lay down with the thistle and
listened to the stones.

SPRING POEM *(after Han Shan)*

My parents left me a pretty fair living
I needn't envy any man his measure

clack clack   that's my muse at her typewriter
yakety-yak   my kids in the garden

the petals come clattering down
my heart capers in his cave

or I sit with my chin on my fist
and listen to the jays

and who comes to my party?
well   sometimes the cat.

WHEN I WAS YOUNG I TRIED TO SING

Whoever I am   the mountains exalt themselves before my eyes
and if I do nothing about the mountains but look at them
they are all I am   what fills these trouser legs
what moves the pen across this page   is mountains.

The colts tumble into the field on their implausible legs
wheel and wait for the mares   feinting at the timothy
so my eyes have gone running ahead   they stand peacefully
drinking the grass   we are all   the colts   my eyes
these shoes   waiting for the mares.

I catch a glimpse of the man who wears my shoes
before whom the trees line up with their backs to the mountain
and the mountain peacefully sets his hair aflame   I tune in
on his pleasure   it is pleasure itself to hear his veins
singing   I am moved easily these days.

His pleasure keeps running ahead   my eyes know where
the colts are hiding behind his shoes   the timothy
trembles in the windy shadow   no light but the
mountain's burning hair   we watch the trees
assemble in the moon   the grass lift up
her million silver tongues   and the mares
the mares drinking it in   drinking it in.

WATER MUSIC

1

"What crime have I committed?" asked Arion.
"You are too rich," replied the captain.

At song's length I held them   sullen as wolves
lashed by music   my arms   my scorpion
my scourge   rooted   an hour they stood
a spinney of thorn-trees

                          tar-handed babies
itching under their beards   resentment flickered
behind their eyes like lantern flames

                              though
what I had done escaped me   twice over
boarding and leaving   I paid for that
passage

        (for them no passage   home was a
drunken island   weaving from harbor to
harbor   panthers prowling the cordage
I the true trespasser)

                nor was it
gold they were after   but my sweet breath
and I gave it   a blast of dithyrambs
all but quenched their flame   I rained down
vowels on their heads   I doused them with
consonants

                      the song is fear   from the
                      gland of alarm   blacker and
                      tinier than a wingless fly
                      spills down my tributaries
                      a flood unstinting   of chill

sea water
              a pool gathers
on the floor of my belly
swells in my throat   from my
mouth gaping   a wound of water
sheathed in quicksilver   I
give birth to her   mother
fear

              fully armed she
darts in their startled faces
her bright ineffectual spear

in a market of thieves I traded gold for
minutes   bought   one note at a time
a song for my last supper   stood at the railing
spitting gold in their faces

dry, stiff, and afraid

              one caught
a note in his teeth to try it   dropped it
for another   trapped in the tendrils of
avarice

              for what?   for one last
burning swallow of sun
my dry soul   hunches like
a miser   the stolen ember
singing in the reed   warms
not at all

that too I thought to render   my will and
testament   the blazing air

              for which was yet

Water Music

Periander   ill used   ill bred   a villain
till (forgiving all   whose hands are clean?)
I flung them my last breath and leapt
in the flood?

2

        "Let us come together here!"
        "Let us come together here!" repeated Echo, and joyfully
        rushed from her hiding place

                Flaring distance   father
                breath   the waves are
                your idea   the idea of
                water is calm   dead
                calm and

launched on the passage   no one pays for
beyond the troubled border   beyond
the wildest dream of light   I passed
twice   going and coming   each time
for good

        The waters compassed me about, even to the soul: the depth
        closed me round about, the weeds were wrapped about my
        head.

        the hall was strewn with
celebrants   some to feast   some
to be feasted on   all of them mannerly
solemn as monks or thieves

                yet I heard
the herring flick past the teeth of
the shark   felt her slip with equal

grace   down his throat   a banquet of
good nature

          enough to go round   who
          sniffs my parting heel as I
          fall from that place?

     *There are some 20 U.S. governmental agencies alone that
deal with the sea.*

          an unaccustomed lightness
          in my lungs   as if my soul
          had finally left and taken
          my body   sodden with
          sleep   when

I felt her nose in my absent lap

          I reached
for my corpse and pulled it on   inside
cringing   colder and hungrier than ever
my soul crowed:

          wake up!   this dream is
yours to ride   asleep you're hers   get
up and wrap your legs around her throat

          shoot to the surface   gasping
          raw light searing the gullet
          my soul cries out as the ember
          blooms again

the ship reeled off on the primal soup
like a drunken crust   I turned
a gobbet even the sea couldn't swallow
to face my savior

grinning   naked as a
goddess   leaping clear   dripping pearls
sleek as a needle   stitching the wind
and water.

3

*His arms and legs were exhausted, his beautiful eyes were
closing, and he would have died if the little mermaid had
not come to help him. She held his head above water, and
let the waves take them wherever the waves went.*

But she could not hold me   she had no
hands!   abashed I fell back

                    a passage
straiter than the last   till shyly she
rolled under me   belly up

                    a sunlit
interval   breathing   cupped in those
fatuous paddles   that fluttering tail

*—simply by signing the agreement. The value of this prop-
erty is incalculable*

                    gone!

                    then at my feet
sweet sibling!   greedy
as I   sucking the wind's
dry tit

and under me
again   wallowing in the
rumpled sheets of the sea

test drilling in "whale pasture"—the oilmen's term

that is to say, they come side by side, male and female, and
mate, and the act extends over a time which is neither very
short nor very long

later   as the sun lay on the wave his
ardent cheek   I threw my arm across
her pliant shoulder   fingers bloodless
wrinkled as wax   clutching her rubbery
stump

      and drifted   flank to flank
into the night

No colt for its rider is so tender of mouth and so obedient
to the curved bit; no dog trained to the bidding of the hunter
is so obedient to follow where he leads; nay, nor servants are
so obedient, when their master bids, to do his will willingly

Love lifted me,
Love lifted me,
From the waters lifted me,
Saved am I.

4

that in the stomach of one Delphinus delphii *he counted the*
ear stones of 7596 little fishes

No moon   only water whispering to the wind
tranced like all doomed pairs in their trivial
exchanges   trinkets of rain   baubles of breath

Water Music

from the lips of drowning sailors
                                    but music
cannot long abide a vacuum   into the kingdom
my voice abandoned   she sent

                    twittering   wailing   whistling
                    groaning   creak of cordage
                    grunt of canvas   rasping
                    clacking

        a high-pitched wavering squeal, like an elfin siren

        Was it an airplane?
        Is it noise?
        Is it music?
        Is it softer than before?
        Is it supersonic?
        When will it stop?

a stream of outlandish colonists   my teeth
moaned softly in my skull   I the true
stranger   out of my element   yielded
at once

            I bowed my head on that
tranquil shoulder   slept like an embryo
rocking in the troughs of her song

                    my ear's awash in her cantata!
                    the water darkens my wit
                    like wine

                            her clicks
                    points of flame   stars in
                    the trackless night   her
                    screams trace pathways
                    everywhere   bounding nothing
                    her grunt punches a hole
                    in the sea

109

I hear the
derelicts dance on the
shuddering floor   the coral
foliage tremble   I hear
the resonant shores reply

black angel   her own harp   all
night   for my sweet sake   she played
herself

and bore my mortal weight
her own mellifluous dory   her own lance
her shield   (against what adversary?)
her mansion   her lithe empire

With what porpoise?

locus of energies   restless
as a wave   spontaneous
but for my sake

(couldn't
let go if I wanted   my hand's
rebelled   he's captain now
I follow meekly   mute as a
stump)

trailing behind her   a great white
albatross   blunting her style   a clumsy
beast we made   a forced awkward joy.

5

*It is not known for what reason they run themselves aground
on dry land; at all events, it is said that they do so at times,
and for no obvious reason.*

When the old man lifted from the billows his fiery
brow   he found   nailed face down in the sand his
prodigal son   the last regretful wavelet kissing
my toes farewell

                        my hands   flung wide
clenched broken shells   the isthmus ground
his gritty knuckle in my ribs

                            (nothing personal
numberless   coarse   long-suffering
the sand-grains bore me up)

                                        he's scowling   can feel his
                                        glare between my shoulderblades
                                        a mouthful of sand for
                                        breakfast   the blood begins
                                        to stir   it's good to be home

        A sigh was the only sign of her deep distress, for a mermaid
        cannot cry.

noon before I heard her   she'd never left
her anguish brought me back to my imbecile
feet

        the horizon reeled

                            the gulls
fell   screaming into the bay

                              gamely she
scaled the glittering cliffs   to catch me

                                  topples back   I stretch my
                                  fruitless arms and drop
                                  to my knees

III

there we dallied   while father paced the sky
the little waves ran back and forth between us
bearing frothy billets-doux

> *"Thou hast a human soul," she answered. "If only thou*
> *wouldst send away thy soul"*

                                    ....   (but he scampered
back from the water   flapping his scraggy
hands   bawling:

                        after him!   now before
he's gone   stalking through the western trees
carry me   body my wayward beast   we'll
ride him down!)

                              by the new moon's
slender light I gathered stones   sea-smooth
transfigured branches   for a fire

                        no use   wade out
                        lie down in the shallows
                        winding my insatiable
                        arms about her

> *Then, "Lift!" shouted the dreamer, and the ponderous black*
> *shapes were half-dragged, half-carried, unresisting, to the lip*
> *of the tide. There they settled down, those beautiful, digni-*
> *fied shapes, utterly at peace, while all hell broke loose around*
> *them. Men, women and children, leaping and posturing with*
> *shrieks that tore the sky, stripped off their garlands and*
> *flung them around the still bodies, in a sudden dreadful fury*
> *of boastfulness and derision. My mind still shrinks from that*
> *last scene—*

> *two years later, Townsend wrote sadly that all his cetaceans*
> *had died. Their death, he said, was clearly due to "keeping*
> *the animals in water charged with sewage."*

There are 130,000,000 square miles of deep ocean to fight in. The ocean floor is furrowed with trenches in which weapons can be hidden

—the largest new block of territory since the Louisiana Purchase

a murky, three-dimensional combat zone.

6

And the surf took it from the waves, and the foam took it from the surf, and the shore received it, and lying at his feet the young Fisherman saw the body of the little Mermaid.

Desolate I gathered tatters of damp seaweed
wrapped her defenseless flesh   to keep from
his prurient eye   in my pitiful hands
brought back   a token of water   my
salt tears

        and saw her   under the
dawn's first glancing blow

                  wince
rise on her flukes   like two black
misbegotten feet

          and take   cow-eyes
aflutter   in her slime-green gown
reaching to me her diffident stumps her
first uncertain steps   across the
broken shells

her threshold for detection of "unpleasantness" in this situation was extremely low

and you Periander   prince
of opposable fingers   golden
thumb   sign me one last
proclamation:

    let there be
no more hands   let the
work of hands   fall in the
lap of days   let all maps
henceforth   be drawn on
water   let there be arms
rather   gentle paddles

no legs either,
Nothing but a torso, and a tail extending
Like a moon's horns, between half-moon and a crescent

she tottered into every ditch   lay down
dabbled in the ooze
    I plucked her out

too soon

it's fatal   but she comes
I can't slow down   I am
what I am

The gradual drying up of the water by the fire is a good
example of what Anaximander meant by "injustice."

what scourged her flesh   replenished mine
what drained her ghost   my soul devoured
what quickened me   set her aflame

whenever we hurt her, she would emit distress calls. This
turned out to be a useful indicator for the experiment.

I run ahead   find the
road!   come panting back
an anxious hound

        past
sniggering children   past
the insolent idiot leer of
yokels and mercenaries   over
the bleeding stones she hobbles
the hours break like truncheons
across her back

We must now point out that there are two categories of
people who undergo torture:
   1) Those who know something.
   2) Those who know nothing.

the old man feasted on her   swilled her
least breath   great festering wounds
bloomed on her back like bloody flowers
odor of myrrh and ambergris   troubled
the air

Each time she shook off the mask, she picked it up in her
teeth and obligingly brought it back to her tormentors.

You must therefore weigh as heavily as you can upon the
body of your torturer in order that his soul, lost in some
byway, may finally find once more its universal dimension.

    then one last time   at the
gate of the city   she paused   quivering
leant her corpse against a tree   and died

    for a fire   for a cup
    in my hand   for a book
    on my knees   a cat
    at my feet

*Personally, I am neither good nor bad. I oscillate, if I may
say so. Also, I've never really done anyone any harm—nor
any good, to boot.*

                            the crime is
    comfort   the node of pleasure
    throbbing   dim as an ember
    banked with ashes

fuddled   the old sot spewed her blood
on the waters   sank to sleep   the last
cart groaned through the wall   the moon
caught her bright horns in the tremulous
branches   the tree took light

*After this, men can believe in anything. They can expect
anything. Be not astonished any more, although you see
beasts of the dry land exchange with dolphins, and assume their place
in the watery pastures of the sea, and beasts who loved the hills
find the ocean's crashing waters sweeter than the bulk of land.*

    in every fountain   I hear
    her voice   my face from
    every flittering pool   gleams
    darkly back

        let there be
    no more eyes Periander   no
    signatures   no history
    martyrs   thrones   no gallows
    banks cathedrals houses
    shoes

        let there be no
    more feet   let there be
    no location   no land beyond
    the sway of water   let there
    be no boats either   only

Water Music

       cold, comfortable sea-water

lapped in the moon's unquenchable flame
never more radiant   black as ice
sublimely passionate   she rose
a constellation of transcendent rage

                the crime is peace

                          the crime
           is what I have   the crime's
           myself.

FROM

A Mote in Heaven's Eye

DISTANCES

1

A man and a cat keep a room
his mark is on the door
the cat's is on the carpet
the bed the radiator
the cat leaps to the table
strolls across the paper
the man is reading
or staring out the window
his thoughtless hand
falls on the cat
asleep on the sill
his fingers drift through dreaming fur

it blinks
stretches
it's time
to go out

2

The man is setting the pace
steadily
gravely
it is his part of the business
gazing neither left nor right

where the cat looks after the shadow
sees to the ashes
discreetly
neither too near nor too far
keeping the distance

3

Rounding the final corner
they part in sight of the door
without ceremony
without valediction

the man goes in
sits down at the table
smooths with his dreaming fingers
the evening's news

hours later
groans to his feet
opens the door
and
thrusting against his leg
as if after all
two bodies might
inhabit the same space
at the same time
the cat comes in

WHO GOES THERE

The lark wakes up with a lousy taste in his mouth
his morning song is a marvel of malediction
he wheels on his sweeter half
she ducks to breakfast
an absent peck beside her beak and he's off to work
Int.   do your worst! come if you dare! come on!

the air's thick with recrimination
a tilting ground of harmony
hymns of discord canons of property
anthems of real estate
his neighbor hurls a diatribe as he passes
like a melodious gauntlet
he stoops to pick it up
Int.   do your worst! come if you dare! come on!

the puppy's yelping in the bedroom window
he's left his mark on the rug
when mistress comes he'll belly up
his tail between his legs
the finch lets fly a mean arpeggio at the mantelpiece
he's master of his cage
Int.   do your worst! come if you dare! come on!

the doves are strutting their ramparts
muttering curses
the sparrow blusters in the hedge
I scowl at the cop
bare my teeth at the secretary
stalk to my pigeon hole
warbling under my breath
some notes of my own
Int.   do your worst! come if you dare! come on!

THEY

are at the end of our street now cutting down trees
a scream like a seven foot locust
they have cut off another
neatly at the pavement
never again will the pin-oak threaten a taxi
will the ash lie in wait to fall on a child

it is a good time for this
the sun is bright
the plane has only just begun
to sprout little shoots from under her fingernails
never again will she dance
her terrible saraband in the tornado
the sweet gum trembles
bristling with tiny mines like brown sea urchins
never again will he drop them on the walk
to menace the sensible shoes of mailmen

they have brought a machine that eats trees
that shits sawdust
they cut off limbs to feed it
snarling it chews the pale green fingers of the plane
the pin-oak's wrinkled elbows and knees
they fill truck after truck with the dust
in the schoolyard now they are cutting down the children
I hear their screams
first at the ankles
it is nothing then to sever
their soles from the asphalt
there is no danger their falling
on the school and crushing it

I have invented a machine that shoots words
I type faster and faster
I cannot keep up with them
in front of the house now they are cutting the rosebush
vainly she scratches their hands like a drowning kitten

they are cutting the grass
scythes in their wheels they race over our lawn
flashing in the sun like the chariots of the barbarians
the grass blades huddle whimpering
there is no place to go
it is spring and the street is alive
with the clamor of motors
the laughter of saws

THE CANE

In the beginning the cane asked little enough
a firm hand
a few soft words
a place by the fire
in return for which
wherever its master went
it went before
crying *Here comes the blind man*
yielding with good grace under his weight
at the crosswalk
saving him once or twice
till one afternoon it paused
mid-stride
its nose to a crack in the pavement
and took root

life seethes in those obscene interstices
those mossy bottoms
even the blind man caught it
the scent of freedom
a thousand rank gardenias
mangoes sour as a drunkard's vomit
it was too late

though he tore it free
though it came to its senses
already repentant
though it mended its pace
though it lay at his feet all night
by dawn it had forgotten again
fawning for a walk

but the blind man has hardened his heart
though it lies by the door all day
with its nose to the crack
he will not take it out

NOTHING AT ALL

A cellar and an attic are friends
the cellar works hard for his keep
and has for his pains a furnace in his throat
and a bellyful of boiling water
the attic sits in the clouds from morning to night
with nothing at all in his head
but a rocking horse and a broken chair

from time to time the attic speaks of going away
sick of the bickering maples
sick of distance
sick of the gaping sky
he would get a place in the city
How can you bear me he sighs

the cellar shrugs *No no*
it's nothing at all
he wallows in the earth
like an ark of stone in a windless sea
nor will he take the attic seriously

one night a storm comes bellowing down from the hills
looking for trouble
its mane crackles with flame
rain drools from its jowls
it takes the house in its teeth and shakes it
from side
to side

a while the friends hold fast
but the attic
weak from want of exercise
lets go in the end
rising like a bat on great ungainly wings
he clatters away over the horrified maples

in time the storm grows bored and mutters off
the cellar crouches in the cooling mire

the fire in his throat is out
his belly gives him peace at last
but through the cracks he watches the sky
for the first time open
its clear blue idiot eye
and sees to the back of heaven
nothing at all
not a sheltering cloud
not a shadow
not a broken chair
the maples drop a few last tears and doze in the sun

NOT SO THE CHAIRS

The tables slept on their feet
like horses
could wait there
forever if commanded
no matter what men set on them
a strong back was all it took
and a little patience

the beds never got up at all
pampered in linens
sprawling in perfumed chambers
while on their breasts the gentry
shrieked and sweated
muffling from time to time a sigh
with a diffident pillow

once in a long while a mirror
might lift a negligent arm
or brush dust from a sleeve
merely to lapse in an absent smile
against the entry wall
a portrait of discretion

not so the chairs
no wonder at first so few appeared
only a king could afford one
set cross-legged on a stone
at the end of the hall
his master ground the royal haunches
in his lap
after an hour
all circulation ceased

later in the dark he sat
unflinching as a tree

while silver straight-pins pierced
his meek upholstered thighs
through all of which he made not once out-cry
nor raised an arm in self defense

little wonder now in the night
they bruise our shins with their bony knees
or drive a sinewy shoulder
in the corporate belly
one day they will turn the tables on us
the mirrors will begin to leer in our faces
there is no viper
like an insolent servant

FOR EVERY DOG

there comes a day
this is it
henceforth
there will be no more
collars no more leashes licenses
no more jangling tags
trappings of fealty

MY NAME IS REX
KING OF JACKALS
I BELONG TO SAPIENS
123 GROVEL STREET

henceforth call me Snarl
I belong to my teeth
I live where I sit

you will set me a place at your table
cut me a key of my own
henceforth I will go when I please
in or out
you will chain the cat out front
to the bird bath
throw him a bone
and when you call again *Here Boy*
look out for your throat

LAME ANGEL

Lame Angel slumps at his desk
his basket is empty
but his hand
clasps and unclasps the indifferent air
like an embryo practicing its grip

like an embryo
he practices everything
swimming creeping chinning himself on the cord
even flying in place

under his shirt his downy shoulderblades
throb like a deer's first horns
he scrapes them against his chair

sometimes in high places
he goes to use them
as a one-legged man might run from a burning house
he'll die before they sprout

clenched in his teeth perhaps
a morsel of wind
a worm rehearsing perpetually the life of a butterfly
but a worm to the end

HIS SHADOW

His shadow dogs him
left or right as he turns
or behind
friendly but diffident
gaunt, its ribs are showing
what does it want

he hurries down his street
afraid to look back
if he looks now it will never go away
he will reach out and scratch its ears
it will lie at his feet forever
licking his wretched shoes
with its soft grey tongue

SOME OF THE SHOTS WILL MAKE YOU GASP ALOUD

He sits in the window grinding
his groin with his horny fist
leafing through batches of LUST
and SNATCH and NAKED MOTHER

Lame Angel has exhausted
the tireless go-go girls
he is learning to read

HOW JUST IN DAYS YOU CAN ACQUIRE THE
HIDDEN SECRETS OF 5000 YEARS OF
RUTHLESS TERROR

from the merci-
less Nahutian Indians, to the Foot Fighters of the French
Underworld

FREE FREE FREE FREE FREE FREE FREE
R   E
E   try the fantastic   R
E   F

FRENCH

F   E
R   E X T E N S I O N E
E   R
E   F

Flips
open in-
stantly and
locks auto-
matically to
prevent acci-
dental closing.
Razor sharp
tough stainless

Over 200
pages on the
pleasures of pain

SIBYL'S LEAVES

Weighted with wrongs his briefcase rolls
inches above the ground
on invisible rails
wind lifts with his cold nose
the skirts of his topcoat

Sibyl waves from her door
in her plastic wrapper
a beer in her fist
a filter king in her teeth
trailing ashes and catastrophe

if there were nothing to fear
his flesh would invent it
he stoops to read the fallen leaves
before he can make out their scrawl
wind turns all the pages

NEW LEAF

Patron of alleycats and suicides
Lame Angel has applied for a government grant
a folder of letters clippings
a list of good works in triplicate

he is learning to smile
not a good smile
the smile of a cripple
though he has little cause to complain
good health good teeth
a reasonable living
and lord knows all angels were not
created equal

BRICKS

The people of the north live in trees
the beams of their houses are cedar
the rafters fir

these people live in caves
cool walls of clay
the rooftree clay

carved from the hill's side
clumsy, uncompromising
all business and corners

scorched in the fire
the colors remember the flame
rust orange salmon inanimate rose

their fathers drove away the trees
only the crippled mesquite remains
good for nothing but the fire

their days are graceless
hard, identical
nights sudden and cold as knives

they huddle, dimly
the wick of reason lowered
a flickering fringe

it is their blood that glows
their laughter
harrowing the shadow

it is their flesh
that smoulders
blackening the ceiling

THE BARGAIN

The man carrying bricks
climbs past our window again
the bricks ride jostling in a sling on his back
flushed, arrogant
craning like tourists
they take the bloom off breakfast

he's set the band across his brow
incurious, he looks neither at us
nor where he's going
but at his desolate shoes

we know where he's going
the bricks have hired him
they come from down there
they want to see the sky
they all shook hands on the bargain
we do not enter

ascending, ascending
he thrusts his brow
against the load of ungrateful clay
we sit where we are
hands heavy with bread

THE STRANGER

On a bench in the plaza
under the barbarous trees
I chew my thumb and watch the girls go round
one way
the boys the other
a stranger in a town of strangers

in the market a man is selling his hands
they hang from his shirt like shameful meat
between us this uneasy peace
if he won't look in my pocket
I won't stare at his sleeves

the label in my shirt says
Do not maltreat me
I should paint it on my hat

and what are the children crying
the consonants spill from their tongues
like streams of colored pebbles
the names of their vowels are Warbler
Linnet Nightingale and Dove
here at last
I can say what I mean without fear
of being understood

ALMS

for Amy

His knees drawn up to let me pass
he is small and miserable
as any man

his stick lies meek at his side
if he speaks it will rise and strike at the walk
pity will drool from the paving stones

he rattles a cupful of furious pencils
each one sharpened to its point
he holds out his fabulous sockets for me
to fill with silver

raptly my right good hand
like an enchanted eel
glides through my pocket
sweetness blooms in my heart and dies
a rose of blood
and for an instant I have more than I need

GENEALOGY

Fire was first
out of fire came fist
out of fist, teeth

teeth begat mouth
and mouth, stone
stone begat worm

worm took his tail in his mouth
and wind was born
out of wind came foot

foot begat running
running, water
water, womb

then
out of womb sprang meat
and meat went into his mother

and begat
and begat
and begat

IF HE COULD

I've tied my reason over my eyes
dog trails at my heels through the weeds

dog never asks *Why?*
only *Now?*
never *Where are we going?*
he drops his tail and follows his nose

if I could loosen with my miraculous forepaws
the furious knot at the back of my head
I'd tear the reason from my eyes
and send it flying

Now now dog would bark
look where you're going
this is the garden
there is the wall

Now he would howl
this is the beginning
here is the tree
give it a name
Earth-finger
Moon-beard, Sparrow-mother

here is the fruit
call it Good
the leaf, Green-tongue
Sky-feather
the sky, Star-meadow
where the dead worm flies
through the voice of the lark

if he could, dog would
And last he would say

If He Could

       name me again
       Hail-fellow, Fast-companion

       Brother
       give you good morning

FINDERS KEEPERS

In that tribe the priests are chosen
for memory alone
they have forgotten nothing
can give the gods their testimony
twelve nights running
chanting to each of the four winds in turn
that none be insulted

whereas the poets have memories
so frail
rising they remember neither
the nightmare nor the night before
wake without history
forebears
crying
ma ma
a lamb on a stone

each day
they construct anew
not merely their own
truncated lives
but the language of the tribe

LILITH

She hissed in my ear
What can you lose?
she wasn't bad
but for the nose
that battle axe
long loose black hair
black arrogant eyes
generous mouth
great creamy boobs
on the frame of a boy
she laid for dwarves
and garbage men
fucked like a snake
beak like a hawk
held open house
in her round bed
without a foot
without a head

where is she now
slithering across what
littered moonscape
stirring with that
irreverent snoot
the dreams of virgins
dry gritty
snatches of spinsters
night lizard
demon of lonely sleepers
while we tumble and turn
in our four square bed
between us a field
a flock a house
two grumbling boys
twenty years
of sweat and bread
and everything to lose

DEUS EX MACHINA

O Hermes 3000
hip grey messenger
god of thieves
what dark conspiratorial vowels
grim consonants
gather in your spools

I'm a god too
look
one stroke of my left hand
the paper rises, radiant
on a hill of keys

I run my fingers
over the white stones
seeking a way in

the paper
stiff, humorless
white as a parson's collar
rides back and forth
in his black carriage
taking notes

INTERVIEW WITH A WINNER

What was it like?
like losing
same bloody feet
blazing tendons
same sweet release
melancholia of exhaustion

What did you win?
a chance

For what?
to do it again
that wasn't it
either

What did you get?
through

What's left for you?
tomorrow's race

losing is worse

COMING DOWN

All day up here sweating out
the lies that oil the works of love
if I had a million tongues I would lie to the grass

I give earth back nothing but her names
Mountain I mumble
old mouthful of stones
as if that might wake her from her trance

in my skull a red bird I can't name
folds his dark wings
the wind strays absently through the trees
riffling folios of light

all day up here
a local skirmish
strictly a holding action
between my fingers and the ledge

at sundown I descend to you dear heart
astonished to find you beating still

NEXT TIME

When I come back I want to be a rock. LIZA

Weary of uprightness
I would slouch like the cat
I would feign like the possum
hang by my tail like the leaf
lie in the dust like a stone
even as the least of these

surrounded by mirrors I am
always there before me
tired fighting over my shoulder
I would turn like the earth
that wretched stone
would look the cold
green moon in the eye
and sleep a millennium
nuzzled by the rain
licked by the sun

PASSAGE

A carp, I dreamed a thousand years
in a cradle of water
what do I want with these knees?

an eon grunting in the shallows
drunk on ether
a season teaching my fingers to dance

somewhere behind me, time on time
history convulses
the ages of ice flash through my veins

I can smell it, that harsh medicinal light
why not?
next time I'll marry worms and father grass

I wonder what the dust hums
dancing in the sun
a mote in heaven's eye

FLYING SONG

Smoke on the wind
I travel light
my way is flight
my cries are music
a bowl of earth
a burning coal
and at my feet
the blessed weeds
the earth's sweet trash
are all I need

seed on the wind
I go alone
I light where I can
I stir the flowers
with my coal
and drink the smoke
the trash of trash
I'm nowhere long

a bowl for my hearth
the fire my friend
I fly when I can
and damn the cost
I think what I am
I know what I'll be
sweet trash sweet trash
in the roadside dust

What Manner of Beast

THE BEAST IN THE MACHINE

> *To provide social contact, it was first decided that an orangutan, Biji, would live in the language-training situation with Lana.*
> DUANE RUMBAUGH,
> *Language Learning by a Chimpanzee*

Lana scowls at the keyboard
she knows why I call these plastic wafers *keys*
she wonders which one unlocks Biji
and where I have hidden the days of their ignorance
in this plexiglass Eden
tickling, grooming, hugging, sharing
tussling under the Guggenheim tree

> *she was both interfering with Lana's work on the keyboard and restricting Lana's linguistic expressions to requests for the barest necessities*

Please machine give Coke
Please machine give M & M
sagely the monitor blinks, an electronic angel
a relay hisses in the wall
and there is Coke
dark, sweet, stinging her tongue with pleasure
click-click, there is M & M
wafer of eternal bliss, body of the machine
through the plexiglass the banked dispensers glow

but where has she gone
sweet orange Biji
silly irresistible Biji
dangling from the go-bar
brushing the console with her toes?

distracted, Lana taps out *Please machine make movie*
for 30 seconds of Primate Growth and Development

which she knows by heart
her genesis in technicolor
then it's back to the non-stop
night and day commercial of the dispensers

> *Quite possibly the various incentives such as movies
> had held little reward value for Lana as long as she had
> the companionship of another ape.*

Please machine open, she scans the console
for the key to *window*, for a glimpse of the action
east of Eden, in the alleys of Nod
where the technicians stray, white-robed and slim

between the hunger and the monkey chow
lies the machine
between the boredom and the colored slides
the machine, which once
toward morning, she entreated
Please tickle Lana

clapped in her plastic cage, tapping out
telegrams to the remote
elusive genius of the machine
her name and the machine's are one
all she needs is a lab coat and a Ph.D.

OF COURSE

By the time of her fourth cycle, however,
she twice attacked her previously favored
trainers. The actual causes of the attacks
are unknown of course
DAVID PREMACK, *Intelligence in Ape and Man*

When Sarah came into her fullness
she had been seven years from home
laboring in the rational vineyard
having not once laid eyes in all that time
on a male of her own persuasion
till Walnut, bright obliging Walnut, came

she reached through the bars
and clutching him close
took his unfledged peter in her mouth
scrotum and all, whereupon
the trainer whipped out his clipboard and his Flair

> *For a brief period Walnut was used as a contingent*
> *event. On a board outside her cage we wrote such things*
> *as "Sarah is good ⊃ Mary give Sarah Walnut" and the*
> *more explicit "Sarah insert cracker red dish ⊃ Mary*
> *give Sarah Walnut." Instructions of this kind restored*
> *Sarah's work habits.*

there are, of course, alternatives
take Lucy, who married a vacuum cleaner
when her labia bloomed, like some carnivorous flower
she dropped her magazine and plugged him in
ran his gleaming nozzle over her body
switching from SUCK to BLOW

> *until she had what I inferred to be an orgasm (she*
> *laughed, looked happy, and stopped suddenly). She*
> *then turned off the machine, picked up her unfinished*
> *glass of gin and her magazine.*

or take the goose who courted the garbage can
three furious years, he defended his mate
from the garbage men, and danced the triumph dance
under her vacant, battered gaze
mounted her, in season
his wings, his heart aflutter

> *He would never react to greylag calls or even to fe-*
> *males, but if you'd just rattle a piece of metal he would*
> *immediately act as if there were another greylag calling*
> *him in the distance.*

when they carried his lady off for keeps
he watched them flatten her in the crusher
heard her death-rattle, then followed
the garbage-hearse, of course of course
two blocks through the deafening traffic
till he was crushed, himself

LUCY CAT

Nor could she part with it, even
so it might eat, or if she did
could not forbear
to stroke it, as it lapped its cream
or sign to it, in the syntax of possession
Lucy cat, till at last it was sated

seven enchanted months, she trundled it
everywhere, a sentient toy
to practice love upon, or let it
ride her shoulders solemnly
pale angel tiger

Unfortunately, though, one day the cat died.

crouched in the corner of her room
she crucified the afternoon
with screams like none she'd loosed before
then, suddenly struck dumb, approached
the incontrovertible tiny corpse
her forefinger not quite touching its fur
signing one long-drawn elegiac *you*

*She clearly had some understanding that the cat was
dead, never to return, for she never looked for it again*

learning in that instant the grammar of loss
never asked for it

nor uttered its name
till three months later, thumbing a magazine
she came on her image, peering from behind a tree
clutched to its bosom, limp, philosophical
Lucy's cat

an ape's age she stared mutely back
then started signing *Lucy cat* and *Lucy cat*
stroking with both hands sadly, over and over
imaginary whiskers, to which still clung
the frail dust-mice of recollection

THE APE WHO PAINTED

Toward the end of his painting career,
Congo was producing excellent circles, but
nearly always filled them in immediately.
ALEXANDER ALLAND, JR., *The Artistic Animal*

Toward the end the painter was subject to sudden
fits of aimless pacing, sucking the end of his brush
his lips were permanently Indian Red, a pigment
to which he had grown obsessively partial

from time to time he would pause
to examine an apple, turning it
in his long, sensitive fingers, or fish
a dust-mouse gently from under his bed
not a hair displaced
or moon for hours, sprawled on his favorite tire
praying to his thumb

how fortunate we are to have captured on film
this miraculous thumb, in full career
sweeping in a great assured arc from left to right
trailing a gleaming Indian Red parabola
counterclockwise, following its own law
tailing up again, toward its beginning
deftly dividing out from in
then filling carefully the bowl of zero
with precious red, horizon to horizon

toward the end, the painter's cage was strewn
with fallen suns, great bloody periods
pages from some cosmic calendar
while he grew more taciturn than ever

PASSION IN PARADISE

> *For reasons yet undetermined, in 1970 our*
> *main study community began to divide.*
> *Seven males and three females with offspring*
> *established themselves in the southern*
> *(Kahama) part of the home range.*
> JANE GOODALL, "Life and Death at Gombe"

And for reasons yet undetermined
not four years later, a gang of five
fullgrown Kasakela males from the north
caught a single Kahama deep in his own territory
and kicked and pummeled and bit him to death

and next month three Kasakelas did in another
prime Kahama male, then five slew Goliath
while four assaulted Madam Bee, without provocation
and left her daughter shooing flies from her wounds
five days, till she died

> *If they were merely trying to reclaim territory they had*
> *lost, they have certainly succeeded.*

four years of search-and-destroy
and the southern range was liberated
though of the two Kahama females remaining, nothing is said
nor of their offspring, but it is presumed
the United Nations sent in a team of advisers

while for reasons yet undetermined
one Kasakela female, Passion by name
drove off her countrywoman, Gilka
made away with her infant and shared it with her daughters
tearing morsels from its breast
as though it were bush pig or monkey flesh

then Gilka's next-born, Passion's elder daughter
likewise kidnapped, and likewise equally shared
while forty-some armed rebels from Zaire
chugged quietly across the lake
and carried off four graduate students
for reasons equally unclear

> *It is sobering that our new knowledge of chimpanzee*
> *violence compels us to acknowledge that these ape*
> *cousins of ours are even more similar to humans than*
> *we thought before.*

Cain's not alone, beast among beasts
his deeds are deft and murderous as the shark's
his works, like the termite's, towering and transient
his most unnatural act is a freak of nature
malign as a tidal wave or a tornado

bad news from the garden at Gombe
the mark on Passion's brow is intelligence
deadliest of virtues
for rarely the fruit falls wide of the tree

THE STRANGE ONE

I   *These strangers made offer of friendship, whereupon,*
by signs, it was agreed that one of their men should come
in the skiff aboard the ship, while in pledge for him, one
of our men went on land.

MICHAEL LOK, *Account of Martin Frobisher's*
First Voyage to the Arctic

There is no accounting for strangers
preferring his bitter tea, his rancid fish
madeira fled down his imperturbable gullet, leaving
not the least flicker of approval

nor would he sit in the Captain's chair
but rapped it with his knuckles
stroked the table, fingered the pewter dish
touched his tongue to the lens of the Master's glass

They are greatly delighted with any thing that is bright,
or giveth a sound.

for beads, for tiny black fires
without smoke, without heat
for a pair of glasses, for wafers of moon
frozen so fast they will not come
unfrozen, even on his tongue
he would part with his parka

and a nail, for a threepenny nail
he would throw in his pipe
for iron, that bends without breaking
that keeps its edge, that holds
a finer point than bone

seeing Iron they could not forbeare to steal

for iron
that fixed him to fish-pale Kabloona
with a swarm of glittering hooks
he would part with his life

2   *the Captain did wisely foresee that these strange people*
     were not to be trusted

Next time the People hove into view in their great canoes
but would not come near, it was this same stranger
who eased his slim craft past the *Gabriel*'s chains
whereupon the Captain called for a little bell
and dangled it chiming over the side

     but with a short arme

so that when the stranger reached for the music
his benefactor plucked him by the wrist
stunned, incredulous, kayak and all
out of the water and onto the deck
whereupon the People withdrew once more
to their barbarous hovels
and the Captain ordered the mainsails set

as for the stranger, he lived
till they landed in England
then died of a cold he had taken at sea

for a handsaw and a sailmaker's needle
his furs, his kayak, and his life
there is no accounting

in pledge for him I come at last
ambassador of sackcloth, envoy of ashes

paddling my wobbly conscience, I make for the shore
me for the strange one
him for me

ANOTHER MATTER

I   *What knowledge they have of God, or what Idoll they adore, we have no perfect intelligence. I think them rather Anthropophagi, or devourers of mans fleshe then otherwise: for that there is no flesh or fish which they find dead (smell it ever so filthily) but they will eate it*
FROBISHER'S ACCOUNT OF HIS SECOND VOYAGE

From the first encounter, all escaped
but one, huddled in the forestays
scowling like a Tartar
in his bloody skins

now, from the last transaction
this old witch, lost in her furs
like a withered root
when the men first flung her to the deck
they tore her moccasins off to see
if her feet were cloven

very strange and beastly
maggots nuzzling the salmon
seal-guts spread on a stone to dry

bleeding from a scalp-wound, the younger female
croons over an injured girl-child, barely two
hugging to her meager breast, one arm
like a bloody doll

> *our Surgeon meaning to heale her childes arme, applyed salves thereunto. But she not acquainted with such kind of surgery, plucked those salves away, and by continual licking with her own tongue, not much unlike our dogs, healed up the childes arme.*

strange, strange
exceedingly strange
the mother's cheek tattooed in broad blue strokes
her lank locks glistening with blood

2   *The man Salvage formerly taken and she brought to-*
gether, every man with silence desired to behold the
manner of their meeting, which was more worth the
beholding than can be well expressed

A good space they beheld, each one the other
speechlessly, as if the grief of captivity
had riven their tongues

then the young female turned her face to the wall
and crooning, soft as a wounded dove
began to sing

    as though she minded another matter

Ice mother, your light
smiles from the snowcrust
winks at the sun

he trudges past you
brushing your hummocks
with his red knuckles

ice mother, mighty stillness
we drowse on your breast
the long night

through the skin
of your cold blue eye
we fish for our dinner

3   *but being again brought together, the Man broke up the*
silence first, and with a sterne and stayed countenance,
began to tell a long solemne tale

Beside me, one brute fell
an arrow through the spleen
while, of the People, three
died on the beach

yet strove, while their arrows lasted
then gathered Kabloona's arrows
then snatched the arrows
from their wounds, and let those fly

and I saw, from the bow
of this demon canoe
an old man, bleeding
leap from the cliff

and another, I saw
then another, that they should not
be taken, leap
while the rest escaped

> *Whereunto she gave good hearing, and interrupted him*
> *nothing till he had finished, and afterwards being*
> *growne into more familiar acquaintance by speech, they*
> *were turned together*

and together, and together
each rarely out of the other's sight
as if they could not bear to be alone

yet never were they seen, in all that time
to use as man and wife
though she made his bed and dressed his meat

though she nursed him through his final illness
scrupulous as any Christian
she bathed him, crooning
her eyes turned to the wall

> *as though she minded another matter*

BY OUR SIGNS

The stones of this supposed continent with America be
altogether sparkled, and glister in the Sunne like gold:
so likewise doth the sand in the bright water.
HAKLUYT, *The English Voyages*

The dolphin in the plastic hammock
has learned to gurgle *Good morning*
Doctor Lilly through his spiracle
the ape Washoe has learned to curse
in fluent semaphore
by their signs we shall know them

waiting for a sign of the prodigal five
who'd vanished, rowing the *Gabriel*'s skiff
round the stony point
for a sack of sparkle
a fistful of glister

> *They are greatly delighted with any thing that is bright*

all day the Captain held at anchor
all eyes scouring the shore
and next morning, sailing close as he dared
to the cannibals' camp, he sounded
the *Gabriel*'s trumpet, fired off a cannon

by his signs, unequivocal
by his trumpet and gun, they knew him
there rose from the huts
an answering blare of laughter

> *very strange and beastly*

and the Captain swore never again
to make peace with those savages
spoke, from that hour

only the language of reprisal
the laying-on of arms

by our signs they shall know us
I pluck a louse from Washoe's fur
and crack it with my teeth
I swim out, flapping my black plastic tail
crying *Uncle, Uncle*
in clicks and squeals

CARIBOU WOMAN

In my dream her black hands
beckon me through the snowlight
I hear them scrabbling on their scraggy nails
scraping ice from the heather

stumbling over the tundra
I saw one wrench a sprig from the permafrost
like a broken tooth
scored, scabrous knuckles of dwarf-pine
lashed by frost-scars
gnarled, charred, scarified
impervious to flame

afloat in my blue torpor
like a cloud over the cooking hut
I can see now through the smoke-hole
one crow-claw herding a wayward ember
back to the fold

the smoke-tongue licks my eyes, but I can see
the red stars dancing on her sooty shoulders
I can make her out now
flat on her belly like a wingless crow
breathing life into the fire

rousing me from my dream
her left claw gently scrapes my cheek
like a willow twig

gnawing the last of the rancid salmon
by the faltering light round the heather wick
afloat in the last of the caribou tallow
I watch her pluck a smoldering coal
to light her pipe

WASTE

By his guttering wick, the eskimo
strokes with a scrap of caribou hide
the flanks of a burnished ivory bear
slowly the beast begins to glow

even the hammer's stolid face
warms, as the carpenter warms to his task
whose forebears pressured blades of flint
so thin they sliced through April mist
and broke on flowers

no labor is ever lost—the years
rise through the ardent carpenter's roof
shimmering in waves of waste
deep in the steel the atoms dance
beyond the storm, the solemn bear
begins his dance among the stars

THE GARDEN

*in order not to sever him entirely from his country
tastes, he was taken continually to walk in some neigh-
boring gardens*
JEAN-MARC-GASPARD ITARD, *The Wild Boy of Aveyron*

Galumphing in his clumsy shoes
down rational cypress avenues
mown paths, raked gravel walks
between exemplary boxwood hedges
irreproachable topiary
borders of hollyhock and poppy
bedded and weeded, chaste and mannerly
the lush geometry of Luxembourg
that green decorum delighted and soothed him
ravished, tranquilized, enchanted
in the garden enclosed, the child set free

how was it then, when the cold wind moaned
Madame Guerin woke in the night
to hear from Victor's room upstairs
peals of sweet immoderate laughter?

*when the inclemency of the weather drove everybody
from the garden, that was the moment when he chose
to go*

one morning when she went to wake him, Madame
remembers turning the key, as ever
behind her in the lock, at the click she saw him
leap from bed with a tremulous cry
and run to the window, how was it then?

there had been in the night a fall of new snow
below, the garden stretched and yawned
in a shimmering peignoir edged with lace
the child ran laughing to the door

which held, she remembers, and once more
to the window, uttering tiny cries
like a captive bird, then suddenly
in the time it takes to make a wish
he was out the door and down in the garden
scampering barefoot in his nightshirt
tumbling through soft drifts, caressing the privet
shaking the fig tree, catching the blossoms
on his tongue, as the garden rang with laughter

how could she bear to call him back?

THE INVENTION OF O

When he found the kitten and called it *dog*
when he called the eagle *duck*, they thought
he'd made all the names he was going to make

when he crept to the moon-pool on hands and knees
and murmured to the swimming face, *baby*
when he said *fly* to a speck of dust, to his thumb
to a little toad, and the toad flicked its fabulous
tongue, unsaying a fly he hadn't seen

he lifted his head to the moon and called out, O
O, he called

HIS NEED

I did not doubt that if I dared to reveal to this young man the secret of his restlessness and the aim of his desires, an incalculable benefit would have accrued.
JEAN-MARC-GASPARD ITARD, *The Wild Boy of Aveyron*

Three Sundays running in the second year
Madame Guerin woke to hear him
crying in his room, no, calling
as a bird calls from his perch in the first
glimmer of false dawn, *lli lli lli*

three sounds the wild child learned
to fatten his orphan dialect
of mutter and grunt, chuckle and howl
first there was O, which he answered to
like a name, but couldn't bring himself
to say, then *lait,* an infant grace
the Doctor coaxed him to chant over milk
and now this warbling at the brink of light
this sweet unmeditated *lli lli lli*

how many Sundays was it, Julie
had joined them for dinner? her faultless Julie
of the downcast eyes, the forthright breasts
that could impale a saint, provoke
not a sound, but a psalm of longing
a song such as infant Solomon
might croon in his cradle, *Julie Julie*

I have seen him in a company of women attempting to relieve his uneasiness by sitting beside one of them and gently taking hold of her hand, her arms and her knees

no more, that meek charade once over
he thrust her away and sought another
soft, recalcitrant shape, and another

till, gently taking hold of her hand
he drew one woman into the alcove
circled her pensively, then flung his arms round her
slender, sinewy, half savage, half boy

she was the last he ever touched
till the day of his death, but for Madame
and that was only when she had been
away too long, he'd cling to her
shuddering like a child who'd given up hope

> *this resignation has served only to exasperate him and*
> *has led the unfortunate creature to find nothing but a*
> *cause for despair in an imperious need*

for all the Doctor's soothing baths
and violent exercise, the storm
in Victor gathered, tossing him
from agony to grief to rage

one morning he sank his teeth in her hand
the tempest guttered like a candle
aghast, he knelt to kiss the wound
his wild heart fluttering in its cage
blood trickling thickly from nostril and ear

> *on the other hand, suppose I had been permitted to try*
> *such an experiment, would I not have been afraid to*
> *make known to our savage a need which he would have*
> *sought to satisfy as publicly as his other wants and*
> *which would have led him to acts of revolting indecency*

her husband dead these twenty years
her man-boy dead at forty-three
one week now, in the tiny house
Madame remembers, what was the pretext?
pressing her ear to Victor's door
remembers the latch-key turning slowly

His Need

so many years and lives ago
how, hunched on his bed, stroking his lonely
half-boy-half-man-root, he gazed
across the altar of his need

what does the Doctor know of need?
three times this week alone she's waked
in the empty house, to nothing at all
to a cry like a fishbone caught in her throat
Victor Victor Victor Victor

THE WORK OF AN INSTANT

For an instant I glimpse her
through the moonstruck tuna
milling and thrashing
she is composed now
under the jostling
one flipper snared in the senseless mesh

the lunatic silver curtain closes
beside me my father
breathless, half-spent
half the catch still to be stowed below
raises his bloody truncheon
his wet black hip-boots
gleam like a fearfully cloven tail

the wicked moonlight
winks at the tip of my grappling hook
as I plunge it into the frantic fabric
it's only the work of an instant
to free her

and lightyears before
I lose sight of her
sinking among gull-scraps
wearing the old imperturbable smile
unresisting, a goddess of garbage
the word made meat

WHALE CANTICLE

The song appears to be evolving.
ROGER PAYNE, *Humpbacks: Their Mysterious Songs*

Late March, the last vast shapes appear
grazing the pack off Cape Adare
sifting the dark all austral summer
ruminating the same long thought

as the new green rubbery ice appears
in the indigo lanes, one matriarch
muses, how nice it must be north
this time of year at Barrier Reef
it's barely a month before she blows

in the chill grey noon her spume appears
to hang an instant, glimmering dimly
a bush of needles on the long low swell

by May on the Reef fat calves appear
cavorting in the rings their mothers make
their elf-cries lapped by the widening rings
of the song, as one by one they all
take up where they left off last year

wrapped in that music, some appear
to be keeping time with their barnacle-
crusted flippers, but never together
each in her own sweet time, now one
perfects the second theme, another
tries it on, as the canticle
takes shape in the warm blue wave, how nice
they never get all of it right at once

THE ONE-EYED CAT

Stalking the stony terraces
dressed in nothing but my lives
it's height I need
I'm only happy out on a limb

june-wind licks white combers of boneset
and queen-anne's-lace
the spruces shrug their dust-blue shawls
and look away

a nestling dangles from my teeth
the grackles swoop and scream
nothing can touch me
but the wind

MOCKINGBIRD CANTATA

A jay's here, here
comes a cardinal, one
fat robin, fooling
neither other robins
nor myself, look out
for the auk, for the auk!

I'm shameless, a nightingale
of weeds, I know, a cardinal
could say it better in his sleep
an unfledged jay
screams more sweetly than I

but I run through thirteen breezy
versions from my aluminum
balcony without missing a beat
while the jay goes on complaining
while the sparrows natter, only
the other mockingbirds
are mute

WEEDS

I have no quarrel with bindweed
when I was a boy
dandelion was king of the gypsies
grinning in the park
through his sooty teeth

nettle and milkweed
burdock, chicory

the weeds move in
an army of poor relatives
shouldering the gladioli

boneset, heal-all
meadowsweet, mother of aspirin

and the weeds move out
impudent garlic the Greeks
called Stinking Rose
chewed against drunkenness
head colds strangers worms the plague
misses her shiftless cousins

goat's-beard, sow-thistle
daisy and mullein

she sidles to the roadside
and sticks out her thumb

all through the winter goldfinch dines
at thistle's table

SHHH

Listen, shhh
alone among trees
I've come for a heart-to-heart
with the woods
I fall on my knees
for a tête à tête with a geode

behind his limestone brow I sense
the clean hard corners of his thought
facet to facet, glinting dimly
postulates of amethyst and quartz

it's small talk time
I'll parley with the loam
make peace with the Indian Pipe
I'll learn to speak weedish

The Detachable Man

CONCERNING THE TRANSMISSION

You might say the same of poetry:
you've sunk too much in it
to quit now, driving
good hours after bad
too much of you wound
round the wires and the hoses.

You might stop addressing
this absence beside you,
cursing through the intricate
cities, singing in the high passes,
tooling down freeways,
minding the numbers,
ears pricked for oracular
tappings, limping past fields
of sullen junkers, eyeholes crawling
with nettle and goldenrod.

If you let go now, the bearings
will scream from their orbits,
the rocker arms clang in their cylinders
and the needles return to their various zeroes,
as if your hands had never clenched
this sweaty wheel.

LEAVINGS

1

Tied in her iron crib like a withered baby,
sinking through infancy as if
she would come unborn, Mother shakes
the I-V clip in her fist like a tinker toy
and thrashes at her bandages, revealing
one livid thigh. From this I came.

2

With a ghost cough and a throaty rattle,
to the twitching bluegreen star
on the monitor screen, to the gasp and sigh
of the breathing machine, her blue lips flutter,
her fitful ember breasts the dark.
Bile streams from her nostril into a beaker.
To this return.

3

Last spring she tried to leave
through the rest home window. *Some rest*, she wheezed,
and hailed a patrol car: *Take me to the Hilton, cabby.*
Leaning back, she groped for her purse
and felt her heart snap open, all but empty:
one lime life-saver, shrouded in lint,
two lichen-green pennies to rest on her eyes.

4

There's nothing left for me now but to leave.
On the way to the elevator, history
dissolves behind me down the corridor.
Old scars and trophies, relics, pride, regret:
my losses fall away from me like fruit,
sweetening the worm's hardtack and compost tea.

IT WAS SOMEONE

It was someone she knew,
someone she trusted,
slid back the chain for,
opened her lonely door.

It was someone she didn't know,
opened his heart to her,
showed her the hunger
crouching inside,
lips drawn back
in a shamefaced grin.

Now from its staple
the chain hangs, inviolate.
The latch sleeps serenely,
its one eye open.

Thoughtless and vague on her
much-crumpled comforter,
her eyes admit
dawn and the janitor.

On her pale throat
the thumbs of hunger
have left their print.

OUR WOUNDS

The mongrel licks his thorn-torn forepaw
doggedly, a dithyramb of licking,
an epic of cleansing.
His wound glistens, naked as water,
as unashamed.

We let our wounds skin over,
a crust of desiccated gestures,
old grimaces stiffening into masks
while we look away.

Then we worry them with our thumbnails,
working relentlessly inward from the edges
till at last they bleed.

THE LEFT-HANDED JUGGLER

The left-handed juggler has everything it takes
to reel in those steak-knives whickering past his ears
except dexterity.

Rectitude, he mutters. *Righteousness. By rights.*
Kingdoms teetering on the point of a word,
sharp as a scream,

self-evident as a splinter under a thumbnail. He lets
the fearful helix snicker on. How can he be
right in the head

out there risking his earlobes and his life, and for what?
For three squares and a flop? Right now for once
he'd set things left,

but the terrible cutlery of circumstance
whirls counterclockwise round the right-of-way, caressing
his sinister fingers.

A QUESTION OF MEMORY

Every morning
the doctor with rimless glances
asks her for the date.

Forgetting backward
she disremembers this morning,
then yesterday,

reels in the years,
undoing the web of her life from the outside in.
Last winter hisses behind her brow, erased.

Caught in her mouth, a memory stirs,
the husk of an enormous moth
that crumbles at the touch.

Voracious, inconsolable, she wolfs it down,
croaks at the doctor, *I know your game!*
and scowls at the wall.

Under her door she can see the days
pass in the corridor like empty wheelchairs.
An inmate shuffles past,

dragging his walker like a portable cage.

THE PERILS OF LAUGHTER

> *The term cataplexy literally means "being struck down," and the emotion that evokes it is most frequently laughter.*
>
> NATHANIEL KLEITMAN, *Sleep and Wakefulness*

Out here, in the doldrums,
where the treading is easy,
rising on muffled swells,
peering down the long slow troughs,
the feeblest snigger is fatal,
the least whisper of frolic.

> *Some patients have time to sit or lie down on the floor so that they do not fall.*

All at once the tendons everywhere
desert their posts, yield
in a body, leaving the bones
to fend for themselves,
the spine a string of ivory beads
in a blood pudding.

Sinews unstrung, the flesh
surrenders to the overwhelming
arms of water, even here
On the threshold of a boundless yawn.

> *The patient may be able to ward off an attack of narcolepsy by engaging in some form of activity; an attack of cataplexy, by learning to curb his mirth or, if he cannot suppress his sense of humor, by withdrawing from the company of friends.*

Forsake all crowds,
all weddings, wakes,
housewarmings, balls,

all banquets, carnivals.
Laughter is endemic,
passing from mouth to mouth.

Abstain from festivals,
picnics, pow-wows and symposia,
deadly revels, rank with foul palaver,
unwholesome banter, pestilential laughter.
Keep out of poolrooms,
discotheques, cantinas.
Snickers are lethal, smiles are suicidal.

Renounce fiesta,
shun horse-play,
abandon whoopee.
Even here, far from shore,
riding these measured
solemn, reasonable swells,
I hear the thunder of multitudes,
the ominous rataplan
of cackle and guffaw.

THE LAST HOURS OF PETRONIUS ARBITER

I

Within a few days there fell, one after another, Annaeus Mela, Gaius Ancius Cerealis, Rufrius Crispinus, and Petronius.

TACITUS, *Annals*

If the whirlwind that struck Campania that year,
toppling villas, levelling cottages, mowing
the fields alike of merchant and aristocrat,
appeared republican to its weirdly calm
dispassionate heart, the plague that devastated
the capital was downright democratic.

> *No miasma was discernible in the air. Yet the houses
> were full of corpses, and the streets of funerals. Neither
> sex nor age conferred immunity. Slave or free, all suc-
> cumbed just as suddenly.*

Wives perished on their husbands' fading embers,
daughters on fathers', where two years before
the bones of Rome lay smoldering.
Nor spared that pestilence harlots or cutpurses,
centurions or senators, the great
lay down with the contemptible.

> *But their deaths seemed less tragic; for by dying like
> other men they seemed to be forestalling the emperor's
> bloodthirstiness.*

For Nero's reigning fear, on the other hand,
wasted only the wealthy and the well-favored,
the overly gifted and the too-much-praised.
Grimly imperial, patrician to the end,
like his appetite, the royal paranoia
silenced Piso the dissolute and Seneca the wise,
Quintianus the conspirator and innocent Silanus,
that ill-starred gentleman whose one offense
was to be noble and respectable at once.

2

> *And, you know, I once saw the Sibyl of Cumae in per-*
> *son. She was hanging in a bottle, and when the boys*
> *asked her, 'Sibyl, what do you want?' she said, 'I want*
> *to die.'*
>
> PETRONIUS, *Satyricon*

By Bacchus' puckered scrotum, I confess,
by Nero's tits, by the knout of Priapus,
I shrank behind a pillar, for once dumbstruck,
while those wheyfaced hooligans, in their scrofulous Greek,
like so many scraggy hatchlings, twittered and screeched
the selfsame phrase my daimon whines each dawn
when I kick my slippers off and reel to dreams,
having dipped my wick in every seething crack,
from knuckle-rumped old buggers to rosy-cunted
maids with nipples hard as babies' thumbs.

Let me come clean, old boy. I gaped like a yokel
at that withered harpy, vexed, interrogated,
shrivelled by inquisition, grilled to a scruple,
slumped like a wizened fetus in her jar,
 from which her answer issued, hoarse and dry,
addressed to no one in particular,
my words, Asclytus, mark you, mine precisely:
I want I want I want to die die die.

3
Look, a little to the left, where a razor scar
leers, thin-lipped, through a gap
in the bandages, as the cadaver-jawed
pianist takes one last drag on his coffin nail,

a little to the left, where the thin haze frails
through the VA ward like a disconsolate fugue,
a tad to the left, the astronomer's dodge
to trap dim stars with the naked eye,

a thought to the left, where the infinite
lours through the ravelled fringe of the Milky Way,
where my own death swims from the bright abyss
like a shivering star and snags in a ragged seine

of capillaries in the corner of the eye:
one bright drop rises at the tip of Petronius'
extravagant dagger, where it intersects
the blanched campagna of his wrist.

4

> *Petronius deserves a brief obituary. He spent his days
> sleeping, his nights working and enjoying himself.
> Others achieve fame by energy, Petronius by laziness.*
>
> TACITUS, *Annals*

Curator of pleasure, professor of revels,
counsellor, critic, connoisseur,
godfather Nero's contract on his head,
disdaining equally both hope and fear,
rode to his beachfront villa at Cumae and threw
his last, best festa, ortolan stuffed with fig,
and honeyed dormice rolled in poppy-seed.

> *He severed his own veins. Then, having them bound up
> again when the fancy took him, he talked with his
> friends—but not seriously, or so as to gain a name for
> fortitude.*

Presiding at his stylish wake, he stole
the scissors of Atropos to snip his thread.
Thinned with prime Falernian, the bright blood seeped
through the bandage to the boozy strains of Nero's guard,
while outside the temple of Hercules the Sibyl
dangled deathless in her jar, while a few bored stars
peered down the alleys of Cumae, looking for a party,
and the moon lay down on the sea's cold tongue like an obol.

STROKING THE CAT

> *What one hears at night are not cries of*
> *voluptuousness but of suffering, the howlings*
> *of a beast whom nature has caught in the*
> *trap.* REMY DE GOURMONT

Just when we'd drifted off so peaceably
rising and falling on that tranquil roar,
that apotheosis of breath, your purr,
your claws begin as if of their own accord
to flex themselves in my defenseless thigh.

Even your tool is set with tiny spines.
The act begins with a groan and dies with a scream,
not shamefaced, sheepish, back-to-back like dogs,
but every-which-way, yowling to be free,
snagged on the pitiless brambles of desire.

Grown men in the performance of your rites
ofttimes transfix their innocent instruments
with fish-bones, twigs, pig-bristles, silver awns.
Nor can I bear to put you down myself,
throbbing here in my lap like an engine of pleasure.

My blind thigh twitches in sleep. This peace has thorns.

WHY WE DIDN'T RENT THE CABIN

Because we knew not a single
flower's name, because we had nothing
to say to the tiny vermilion stars
crouching in the nameless green
tangle of weeds, because the burly
gas-cylinder hunched in the underbrush,
a stranger spying on strangers.

Because no asters raised their
customary violet constellations
to guide us to the clearing's edge,
because no columbine shook its
scarlet jester's cap-and-bells
to greet us, no jewelweed nodded
its succulent flamegold corollas.

Because through the farther trees someone
nameless, less strange perhaps than we,
hefting what could only have been
an automatic weapon, sent
round on baffling round into
the dim green side of afternoon.

Backing down the driveway spitting gravel,
trusting the blind curve and the sudden
silence, I felt a tick groping the sunless
hairs of my skin, another nomad seeking
only a quiet meal and a room for the night.

THE MAN ON THE TRAMPOLINE

The man on the trampoline
lets himself down gently
but firmly. He knows
there is a bottom to every season.
He stretches his toes to touch it,
disappearing to the waist.

The web yields,
tightening, tightening,

till he finds the nadir.
Then, toes together,
dancing on a needle,
arms lifted, as in flight,
his white robes billowing
in the sweaty, desolate gymnasium,

he rises from his tomb
toward the star-streaked skylight.

SALISBURY CATHEDRAL FROM THE BISHOP'S GROUND
Constable, 1823

If, by melting or smelting, by roasting
or blasting, solution or dissolution,
they wrought the transmutations of lead,
by precipitation, by flaking or grinding
from greasy slate to chinese scarlet,
from grizzled ash to royal red,

to what might humble lead aspire,
burning yellow, blending green,
that grey stones reach for milky clouds,
that under Salisbury's soaring towers
Constable's cows might safely graze
and meek grass turn to clotted cream?

WHEN THE LIGHTNING STRIKES

You will remember nothing.
You will remember nothing of these
millennia while your hand inexorably
closes round the glass, and your molecules
serenely rearrange themselves.

When I count three and snap, the glass
will fly into shards.
You will unfold from your chair
and slump to the floor like a wounded carp,
thrash away from the open window, leaving
a trail of blood on the carpet
which will dry by morning a poignant umber.

You will remember nothing when you wake.
You will remember wanting only not
to die, not yet,
as they lift you to your feet,
giddy, bleeding, green, original,
raging to alchemize and replicate.

BREATHER IN EDEN

For the chaste blue mountain air
we fled together, dodging villainous semi's,
sixteen hundred miles of implacable cactus.

Now down the Alley of the Dolorous Virgin
a lumbering dump-truck thunders over the cobbles.
The afternoon is drenched in attar of diesel.

Then a jackdaw whets his beak on the TV aerial:
a slim breeze shivers and wakes and the garden's
suddenly sweet with essence of burro dung.

The sun beams down from the blameless sky
on this sinful Eden dripping with unjust desserts.

BRICK-SONG

Gusts of music sweep
from the bricklayers' Philco,
wafting from its black calyx
attar of saxophone,
pheromones of guitar.

From their brick-pink roof
a hodman crows like a gamecock,
a grackle answers.
I'm laved in a sea of palaver,
birds, bells, ching ching
of trowel trimming brick.

They will make, name it,
of brick and fresh mortar,
a chimney, a chapel,
an altar, a three-storey ark
brimming with brick flamingoes
and blushing doves.

They will lay me a ceiling
flat as a mill-pond
and dare me to dance on it.

THE BLUNDER CIRCUS

El Circo Blunder rumbled in last night
and raised a mossgreen tent on the soccer field.
Three yellow semi's debouch
a trickle of wild life, offloading
elephants, ponies, peacocks, anacondas,
the clean and the not-so-clean,
a freakish ark, a convoy of arklets
tacking from peak to peak.

Now through the town
a van called *Blunder* trails a wake
of turbulent children, blaring the word.
The Six Hundred Year Old Man has set up an altar.
He's calling them round:
his wife the contortionist, the clowns his boys,
and their wives the Giantess
and the India Rubber Maid and the Tattooed Lady.

The mannerly lion strolls in with the mangy ape,
the Salamander Girl slithers hand in hand
with the Human Torch—outcasts and innocents,
an alternate seed-world, hybrid, migratory,
four hundred and fifty thousand
stupendous cubits cubed of glitter and roar:
our second chance.

AT THREE A.M. THE DOGS

strike up a tune.
One sounds the downbeat:
what's he caught,
what scent, what inspiration?
The moon smells acrid as always
like cheap regret.

Others pick up the tune now,
each at his own pitch.
Some take the high notes, some the low,
bassos and coloraturas,
one heartfelt phrase, repeat ad nauseam
their dogged oratorio.

The chorus keeps it up
as stars rattle softly in the sky's black calabash.
How classical. How chaste.
To each his own appropriate refrain,
one trenchant epigram to see him through the night
like *thief!* or *don't!* or *mine! mine! mine!*

THE OTHER DOGS

Here they stalk the street
like cats, all bones and business.
Mostly they keep their teeth to themselves.

They know whence cometh
their sustenance, but
mind your shoes.

For a price, one will sit at your gate
and guard your house
from the other dogs.

THE DETACHABLE MAN

SAVORING THE SALT

He takes the cold way home, along the boardwalk,
in the brackish, gaunt Atlantic City dawn.
Beside him in the somnolent casinos
wheels turn dreamily on sea-green tables,
brigades of one-armed bandits hold up morning.

The sea-wind kisses him fiercely, leaving on his lips
the smack of straining rope, of creaking holds,
astringent, keen, a penny for the helmsman,
sour as recollection, shrewd as doubt,
dank as his mother's brow in the midnight ward.

To make good his losses, to replenish his waters:
his daily brine. He runs the tip of his tongue
across the knife-edge of his smile, to take it in.

ELECTION DAY

Up since daybreak, he cast his worm with the earliest birds,
flew down to the grade school gym and exercised
his insufferable right to choose,
among losers, the one least likely to exceed.

One cheer for the off-white knight on the scrawny horse
and the stunted platform: *A pinch of salt in every pot.*
Asperity's around the corner.
Hole in his gauntlet, couldn't sell a Cadillac to an arab.

Mind, not that our citizen's bored.
A tang of civic fervor still kindles his blood,
but the whole bitter day's before him
and the bars are closed.

Not a twig in this twittering city
to roost on for a spell in the glow
of this uncommon communal fever
while it still simmers.

THE PARTY

They're throwing a party upstairs.
He can hear it carom off the walls and fall
on his sweat-streaked ceiling.

Fretful as a splinter, he'd like
to join the party, senator
from the state of dislocation,
his infinitesimal pressure against history
faint as starlight thrumming the hairs
on a general's wrist.

He ascends from his coldwater grotto,
bobs through the flotsam, fetches up
on a stool by the anchovies.
A mermaid stoops to inquire: *What do
you do?* Her baubles dangle
in the weedy shadow.

I feed on air, he smiles,
*like an orchid. I do
with, my delectable sea-grape.
I do without.*

PASSING GO AGAIN

Across Baltic, in the P.O. parking lot,
the mailmen's Pintos line up at the fence
to watch him pass.

The Grand Old Flag droops on its tall white stalk
like a wilted flower.

By the long green windowless hotels,
swathed against sparrows, the seeded lawns
thrust glass-green spicules through their bandages.
From the schoolyard, tiny bright green screams
pierce morning's shawl.
It's a bad day on Atlantic Avenue
and April's just begun.

Still, it's the only game in town.
A bent black yard-man, raking
dead leaves from the privet, meets the ghost of his smile
with a spectral grin.

While the sun hums overhead to the rustle of money
he scoops up his old bones, and shakes them again.

A HOME AWAY

He comes bearing a cluster of subway posies
or a plaster mermaid
for the wife.

Vagrant, avuncular, perpetual uncle,
rapt nephews bring him ale
in golden cans.

Nieces, flushing, wear his pop-tops
for sweetheart rings.
At Sunday brunch with his old war buddy

our errant templar
nuzzles the dregs like a golden carp,
bottom-feeding in the gene pool.

NO NEWS

In the paper tonight it's as he thought. He reads:
The mole has no mating call, although it can make
a couple of sounds that are more or less "conversational."

He contemplates the peacock's wanton scream,
tunes in on the great whale's shameless serenade,
throbbing halfway round the world. A mole of few words,

he plunges through the small talk: *these small sounds*
probably occur when a male and a female mole
stumble into one another. Somewhere, he knows,

a soft grey nymph with moist, myopic eyes
dog-paddles toward him thorugh the fragrant loam.
This moment, the earth might crumble between them,

the last crumbs of topsoil toppling from her velvet nose.

IF PEOPLE HAD ROOTS

When the rivers return to their springs,
when the leaves fly home to their forsaken branches,
when the gypsies go back where they came from,
when the killer revisits the scenes of his innocence,
this eel will wriggle back to his mère
in her seaweed housecoat and shipwreck slippers.
He'll take down his *Almanac of Weeds*
and trace his roots.

Till then he'll persist in his one-man diaspora,
tramping the boondocks with suitcase and six-pack
from wilderness to wilderness,
catching his breath in the villainous cities,
snoring serenely in rented sheets.

If people had roots they'd roost like trees
up to their ankles in earth.
They'd shuck their rags when the north wind called.

METASTASIS

Where is he now? Still drifting,
a cell without a country,
bobbing the arteries of Megalopolis
looking for somewhere harmless to happen.

He passes through airport x-ray portals
like a cosmic particle, passes
roadblocks and customs agents like a gypsy meson,
biding nowhere long.

In a dank hotel in Vera Cruz
he soaks his computer card in sweet white wine,
thoughtfully mutilates a corner,
reloads his empties with lullabies to mermaids
and sends obscene postcards to the editors of *Life*.

*Donald Finkel was born in New York City and
attended public schools there, notably the Bronx High
School of Science. He studied sculpture at the Art
Students League, and after earning a B.S. in philosophy
and an M.A. in English at Columbia left the east for
Illinois, Iowa, and finally St. Louis, Mo., where he
is Poet in Residence at Washington University. He has
lived for several years in Mexico, and travelled widely
in the United States. He is married and has three
children, three cats, and a Border Collie. He has been
the recipient of a Guggenheim Fellowship and a grant
from the National Endowment for the Arts. In 1974
he received the Theodore Roethke Memorial Award
for the book-length poem,* Adequate Earth. *In 1980
he received the Morton Dauwen Zabel Award from
the Academy and Institute of Arts and Letters for*
Endurance *and* Going Under.